WHAT MAKES
CIVILIZATION?

David Wengrow is Professor of Comparative Archaeology at the UCL Institute of Archaeology. He has also held positions at Christ Church, University of Oxford, the Warburg Institute, and the Institute of Fine Arts, New York University. He has conducted fieldwork in Africa and the Middle East, most recently in Iraqi Kurdistan, and writes widely on the early cultures and societies of those regions, including their role in shaping modern political identities.

WHAT MAKES CIVILIZATION?

THE ANCIENT NEAR EAST AND THE FUTURE OF THE WEST

DAVID WENGROW

OXFORD
UNIVERSITY PRESS

OXFORD

UNIVERSITY PRESS

Great Clarendon Street, Oxford, OX2 6DP,
United Kingdom

Oxford University Press is a department of the University of Oxford.
It furthers the University's objective of excellence in research, scholarship,
and education by publishing worldwide. Oxford is a registered trade mark of
Oxford University Press in the UK and in certain other countries

© David Wengrow 2010

The moral rights of the author have been asserted

First published 2010
First published in paperback 2018

Impression: 7

Published in the United States of America by Oxford University Press
198 Madison Avenue, New York, NY 10016, United States of America

British Library Cataloguing in Publication Data
Data available

Library of Congress Cataloging in Publication Data
Data available

ISBN 978-0-19-280580-5 (Hbk.)
ISBN 978-0-19-969942-1 (Pbk.)

Printed in Great Britain by
CPI Group (UK) Ltd, Croydon CR0 4YY

for Abigail, everything is possible...

CONTENTS

LIST OF MAPS AND ILLUSTRATIONS

Maps (Created and Drawn by Mary Shepperson)

Illustrations

1. Gold casing of a cult statue with lapis lazuli inlays around the eyes, from Tell el-Farkha in northern Egypt, *c.*3200 BC ('Late predynastic period').
2. Marble face of a composite figure, with shell and lapis lazuli inlays, from Mari, Syria, *c.*2500 BC.

CHRONOLOGY CHART

Years BC	EGYPT	SYRIA–PALESTINE	MESOPOTAMIA	IRAN	CENTRAL ASIA	PERSIAN GULF	INDUS VALLEY
9000	Hunter-fisher-gatherers (use of pottery across the Sahara)	Pre-Pottery Neolithic (permanent villages, cereal farming, herding of sheep, goat, cattle; maritime spread of farming to Cyprus)			Steppe hunter-gatherers	Hunter-fisher-gatherers	Hunter-fisher-gatherers
8000						rising sea levels ⇢	(domestication of zebu cattle)
7000	Nile Valley Neolithic (mobile herders, Egypt to Khartoum)	Pottery Neolithic				shell middens ⇢ (use of sail?)	Neolithic
6000				(use of seals and painted ceramics; small-scale irrigation in southern Mesopotamia and on the Iranian plateau)			
5000	(cereal farming in Nile Delta, spreads south by 4000 BC)		Ubaid period (complex metalworking, tree crops, wool textiles)		Caucasian Neolithic (horse domestication on Pontic steppe?)	Neolithic (Ubaid maritime links)	
4000 *Spread of plough agriculture across Eurasia, and Egypt*	Predynastic (urbanization, hieroglyphic script)	(sailing along Levantine coast and Red Sea)	Uruk period ⟵ (urbanization, 'Uruk expansion') ⟶ (cuneiform script in southern Mesopotamia)	(pack-donkey and wheeled transport) ⟶	(herding economies, complex metallurgy; wheeled transport)	'Dark Millennium' (site abandonment)	(cereal farming, cattle, sheep, goat herding)
3000	OLD KINGDOM	(Kingdom of Ebla; Byblos trade with Egypt)	EARLY DYNASTIC	Proto-Elamite (urbanization)	Kurgan burials on the steppe BACTRIA-MARGIANA ('oasis' cities)	Umm an-Nar tombs in Oman EARLY DILMUN (urbanization)	HARAPPAN (urbanization, Indus script)
2000	MIDDLE KINGDOM	(Canaanite city-states)	OLD BABYLONIAN	OLD-MIDDLE ELAMITE			
1000	NEW KINGDOM		KASSITE/MIDDLE ASSYRIAN				Ganges hoards

PREFACE AND
ACKNOWLEDGEMENTS (2017)

As a new millennium opens, the people of the Middle East—home to the invention of farming, the first cities, and the creation of the world's earliest literature—face an uncertain future. Devastation and displacement have taken place on a scale not witnessed in Eurasia since World War II. An intricate tapestry of ethnic and religious communities has been unravelled, its ancient threads forced apart. Cherished landscapes of extraordinary age and magnificence have been reduced to rubble; libraries and archives burned; museums and historical sites looted and their contents sold for profit. Many parts of the region have witnessed the decimation of their burgeoning and cosmopolitan middle classes, the hollowing out of their hard-won civil societies. All this unfolds on the doorstep of a European Union in the throes of self-doubt, its frontiers braced against the flow of victims.

Modern history shows that the fate of Europe is inseparable from that of the Middle East. How will future generations regard that relationship? Some political commentators, historians, and social scientists—often the more influential ones—would have us believe that the fragmentation and devolution of the Middle East since the fall of the Ottoman Empire has been a necessary precondition for Europe's rise from a patchwork of principalities to a global superpower. The same authors argue that ongoing isolation of the Middle East and its peoples—currently implemented with unprecedented force in America's new travel restrictions—is a price we must pay for the security of the West. Internal barbarism in Middle Eastern states will continue to be tolerated, even tacitly supported, insofar as it promotes a stable trans-continental flow of natural gas and crude oil; and so long as the region's more militant malcontents can be held at a safe distance (the historical background to these attitudes is addressed in Chapter 1).

However, this 'clash of civilizations'—surely the worst of all worlds—will only become a lasting geo-political reality if we in 'the West' allow the Middle East to become *terra incognita*: a remote, mediatised landscape of ancient relics, modern fanatics, and smouldering oilfields. This book is for those who want to probe deeper into its history, beyond the rise and fall of states, and back to the foundations of civilization. What I mean by 'civilization' in the chapters that follow will be different from most current usages, which define ancient Egypt and Mesopotamia (in the modern countries of Iraq and Syria) as 'early civilizations' by comparing them to other ancient polities, such as those of Shang China or the Classic Maya. What these comparisons really refer to is not civilization, in any literal sense, but rather the rise of centralised government, monarchy, literate bureaucracy, taxation, standing armies, even slavery: in short, the emergence of social and cultural worlds held together by top-down administration and violence.

There is, however, another way of defining civilization, closer to word's Latin root (*civilis*), which refers to the way societies organise themselves through processes of voluntary coalition: civilization from the bottom-up, rather than the top-down. What defines civilization, in this case, is not a political unit (whether kingdom, caliphate, or empire); nor is it a trait list of technological achievements (systems of writing, mathematics, or astronomy, monumental art and architecture, sophisticated metallurgy, the plough, the sail, and so on). Rather it refers to the capacity of societies to form a moral community—an extended field of exchange and interaction—despite differences of ethnicity, language, belief systems, or territorial affiliation. 'Civilizations', in that sense, have a far deeper history in the Middle East than the earliest monarchies and empires; but as I go on to discuss they also provided the cultural milieu from which those ancient superpowers arose.

In Part I of the book I argue that the early societies of Egypt and Mesopotamia—which are usually studied and presented in mutual isolation—in fact arose from a common 'cauldron of civilization'. The choice of term reflects, in part, the importance of cooking practices (always a good barometer of social life) in my account. It also evokes a close interdependence between the kingdoms of the great river valleys and less numerous peoples of the surrounding deserts and highlands. These residents of the mountains, foothills, and plateaus—known to us largely through the wary eyes of their literate neighbours—added new and crucial ingredients to the

cultural mix, supplying precious materials to the popu-
lous cities of the lowlands—metals, minerals, coloured
stones, fine timber, and incense—so that their gods
could be fed and appeased. Following the trail of those
interactions will lead us from the remote highlands of
Afghanistan to the walls of Troy, from the cities of the
Indus Valley to the ports of the Persian Gulf, and into
the inner sanctums of royal power on the floodplains of
the Nile and the Euphrates.

In pursuing these connections, I have left aside the
details of dynastic succession; the rise and fall of kings
and royal lines. While these form the substance and
structure for many other histories of the ancient Near
East, they are of only secondary importance for the kind
attempted here. Additionally, I emphasize continuities
in the unfolding pattern of civilization that transcend
our conventional distinctions between 'prehistory' and
'history' (or non-literate and literate societies). To talk of
civilizations, however, is not just to describe the past. It
is also to reflect on what is different about the societies
we live in, and how they draw from past traditions and
earlier patterns of civilisation. In Part II, I consider the
legacy of the ancient Near East in the modern world,
and particularly its paradoxical place in the Western
imagination—as both the ultimate source of our own
civilization, and its rejected alter ego.

The first edition of this book appeared in 2010.
Sweeping changes throughout the Middle East mean
that its closing sections now have a very different context. In particular, the themes addressed in Chapter 10

('Ruined regimes: Egypt at the Revolution')—while mainly concerned with the formative events of the Napoleonic era—resonate in a new way with the wave of democratic uprisings hailed as the 'Arab Spring', and the suppression of freedoms that followed in most Middle Eastern countries where calls for constitutional reform took place. The other major political development since that time has been the lightning ascendance of a highly organized fundamentalism known as *Daesh* or ISIS (Islamic State of Iraq and Syria). In summer of 2014, as their insurgents were taking control of the city of Mosul, I was in Iraqi Kurdistan, completing a season of excavations near the bustling border town of Halabja. Our project was investigating the beginnings of what this book (Chapter 4) refers to as the era of the 'First Global Village'—that extraordinary period, between the origins of farming and the appearance of the earliest cities, when village-scale societies across the Middle East fostered many of the innovations we now associate with the word 'urbanism'.

After 2014, a steady flow of requests followed for public comment on the destruction of cultural heritage—a core field-policy of ISIS militants—and especially the large-scale attacks inflicted on the World Heritage Site of Palmyra, ancient caravan city, and literary setting for the Comte de Volney's meditations on the "ruins of empire" (Chapter 10). Like many other researchers, I have felt conflicted in my responses. This reticence came into acute focus with the unlikely events of spring 2016 when, immediately after a Russian-backed and, as it would turn out, temporary liberation, Palmyra was suddenly playing host to the Mariinsky Symphony Orchestra. Under ISIS occupation, its Roman theatre had become a stage for gruesome atrocities, including the murder of its leading archaeologist. Now an audience comprising mainly soldiers sat to watch a classical concert, carefully orchestrated to illustrate a certain idea of "civilization" ('cultural heritage for all humanity', in the words of President Putin's live link from Moscow).

Through the ages Palmyra has opened its gates to all manner of foreign gods—Babylonian Bel, Shamash, and Ishtar; Damascene Hadad and his divine consort Atargatis; Baalshamin, Astarte, and Melqart from the city-states of the Phoenician coast. 'Everything', wrote the great historian Mikhail Rostovtzeff, 'is peculiar in the peculiar city of Palmyra'. Yet nothing, perhaps, as peculiar or unforeseen as the events of 2015–16. To myself, as to many others, there seemed nothing "civilized" about playing Prokofiev in the beautiful wreckage of one ancient Syrian city, while the living population of Aleppo, to the north, was simultaneously under attack. Now, perhaps more than ever, the beleaguered remains of the ancient Near East stand as a warning of the sacrifices people will tolerate to preserve their chosen form of life; of the potential for unfettered expansion that exists within any cultural tradition; and the blood that may yet be spilled on the altar of a misguided notion of civilization.

In preparing this new paperback edition of *What Makes Civilization?* I wish to thank the staff and students of the UCL Institute of Archaeology, the most stimulating environment that any researcher could hope for. I remain grateful to Katherine Reeve, Matthew Cotton, and Luciana O'Flaherty at OUP for their editorial assistance; and I extend my appreciation again to the many friends, former teachers, and colleagues who read and commented on the original version of the book, and are named in the original (2010) preface. For their help and encouragement, I am particularly grateful to David Graeber, Eleanor Robson, Melissa Flashman, Louise Martin, and Brenna Hassett, but above all to Ewa Domaradzka for her unwavering belief in the book, and in me.

London, 11th March 2017

INTRODUCTION:
A CLASH OF CIVILIZATIONS?

> Our subject is the birth of civilization in the Near
> East. We shall not, therefore, consider the question
> how civilization in the abstract became possible.
> I do not think there is an answer to that question; in
> any case it is a philosophical rather than a historical
> one. But it may be said that the material we are going
> to discuss has a unique bearing on it all the same.
>
> Henri Frankfort, *The Birth of Civilization in the*
> *Near East* (1951)

> We are now in the middle of a full-blown Jihad,
> that is to say we have against us the fiercest preju-
> dices of a people in a primeval state of civilization
> …We've practically come to the collapse of society
> here and there's little on which you can depend for
> its reconstruction.
>
> From the diaries of Gertrude Bell, Britain's
> Oriental Secretary in Baghdad (1920)

The historian Lucien Febvre once warned that to
seek the origins of 'civilization' is to embark upon a
series of dangerous excavations (*'sondages hasardeux'*).

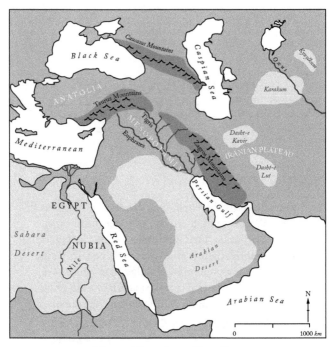

Map 1. The ancient Near East

He was referring to the murky etymology of a word that first entered European languages during the late eighteenth century, in an age of empire and revolution. Its genesis in the philosophical writings of the Enlightenment is elusive. Among the earliest attestations comes in the third volume of Nicolas-Antoine Boulanger's *l'Antiquité dévoilée par ses usages* ('Antiquity Revealed by Its Customs'), a 'critical examination of the main attitudes, ceremonies, and religious and political institutions of the different peoples of the earth'. Posthumously published in 1766, this was one of a number of highly theoretical works in which Boulanger sought to bring order to the complex history of human political relations. An earlier volume, *Recherches sur l'origine du despotisme oriental* (1761) had laid foundations, asserting the existence in Asian societies—both ancient and modern—of a type of political subject alien to Europe: a subject passionately wedded to his own oppression, 'kissing the chains' that bind him, and heroically sacrificing his life at a tyrant's whim. In *l'Antiquité* Boulanger advised the administrators of his day: 'When a savage people has become civilized, we must not put an end to the act of civilization by giving it rigid and irrevocable laws; we must make it look upon the legislation given to it as a form of *continuous civilization*.'

Febvre's choice of archaeological metaphor is apposite. The idea of civilization has always been linked to the desire for universal history; a history that transcends written records, extending back in time to the origins of our species, outwards in space to encompass the full range of contemporary human diversity, and—at least in its early formulations—onwards into some improved future condition. Today we might again be inclined towards the anti-utopian interpretations of civilization that proliferated around the middle of the twentieth century—Sigmund Freud's juxtaposition of culture and sexual fulfilment, or Franz Steiner's dark vision of the West as a society that, through technology, has finally tamed the primeval spirits of the corn and wilderness, only to succeed in driving its demons deep into the heart of society itself. In origin, however, civilization was a profoundly optimistic concept, whose adherents believed fervently in the natural tendency of human history towards a synthesis of scientific reason and moral progress. By 1798, when Napoleon Bonaparte set out to conquer Egypt, it had also become a powerful source of political rhetoric, and a cause worth dying for.

John Headley (2000) has cogently argued that the European notion of human history as a 'civilizing process' of universal dimensions long predates the use of the word civilization itself. He finds it, for example, in Late Renaissance interpretations of the Greco-Roman 'cosmopolis'—a civic community forever coming into being and expanding through its transformation of a barbarian periphery. In adapting the ancient ideas of *polis* and *civitas* Jesuit scholars and administrators of the sixteenth century, such as Giovanni Botero and José de Acosta, found a cultural compass around which to orientate the newly 'discovered' peoples of the non-Christian world. On the basis of technological traits—such as the possession of writing, planned and permanent settlements, monumental masonry, and sophisticated equipment for eating, clothing, and waste disposal—certain pagans were deemed further along the road to full humanity, and hence more prepared for evangelization, than others:

In the *De procuranda Indorum salute* José de Acosta had made the two features of literacy and settlement, but chiefly literacy,

4

the prime determinants for distinguishing different degrees of civilization within the broad category of barbarism. Thus the Chinese as most obviously literate as well as settled recommended themselves in the first category, the Mexicans and Peruvians as settled but only most primitively literate belonged to an intermediate category, whereas such nomadic pre-literate peoples as the Brazilians and Chichimeca revealed a pre-social condition of utter savagery. By defining a measure of civilization religiously neutral according to the determinants of literacy and settlement, Acosta had in effect provided a fragile, slender ledge upon which could be extended the broadly recognized and even admired architectural and social features of the Mexican and Incan peoples.

At the height of nineteenth- and early twentieth-century imperialism, the idea of civilization as a quantity that can be identified to a greater or lesser extent in all human societies achieved the status of scientifically verifiable fact. Racial type—measured and classified on the basis of phenotypical features such as skin colour and skull form—came to be regarded as an accurate indicator of a population or individual's place within the specrum of 'civilized' and 'non-civilized' peoples. The status of the ancient Near East as a 'cradle' or 'birthplace' of civilization was paradoxical in this regard. It reserved an exalted role for this region in the making of the modern world. But it also implied that civilization had since moved on, from ancient Near East to modern West. In the twilight years of the Ottoman Empire, many European visitors to the Near East wrote of its neglect; of the loss of civilization and a subsequent reversion to some more primeval state. The idea of a 'cradle of civilization' also suggested the need for external custodianship of a threatened legacy, imposed by force if necessary (cradles, after all, are occupied by helpless infants, not responsible adults). This was partly a matter of explaining why vast quantities of antiquities needed to be brought to Europe and America for study and safekeeping, but it also resonated with contemporary political affairs (the collapse of Ottoman authority and the growth of European military power in the region), and with the wider intellectual concerns of Victorian scholarship, particularly in matters of race and imperial conquest.

'Civilization', wrote James Henry Breasted (1865–1935)—the founder of Chicago's illustrious Oriental Institute, 'arose in the Orient, and Europe obtained it there.' The history of the Near East could, he argued, be understood as a series of titanic struggles between the Indo-European and Semitic peoples, who converged repeatedly upon the 'Fertile Crescent' of western Asia from their respective homelands on the steppes of central Asia and the deserts of Arabia. The struggle, wrote Breasted in 1916, 'is still going on'. As historian Thomas Scheffler (2003) points out:

Breasted's geo-strategic view of ancient history betrayed some striking parallels to the imperialist zeitgeist of his own times. By and large, the area he designated as the 'Fertile Crescent' was geographically coextensive with those parts of the Ottoman Empire that the Sykes–Picot agreement of 1916 had reserved for Great Britain and France [i.e. the Levantine coast, eastern Anatolia, and Mesopotamia]. By 1916, when *Ancient Times* was published, the USA had not yet entered the First World War, and the King–Crane Commission had not yet submitted its famous report of 28 August 1919, recommending an American mandate for Asia Minor and Syria. Nevertheless, the language Breasted used for describing the Fertile Crescent indicated how much he was aware of the region's pivotal geo-strategic importance, especially for the control of the Persian Gulf and the Red Sea.

Contemporaries of Breasted wrote with conviction about the lack of a warrior caste in the indigenous literary traditions of the ancient Near East, drawing contrasts with the elite fighting bands of Indo-European mythology. It was widely argued that technological prowess in the arts of combat (exemplified by their use of the horse-drawn chariot) allowed these 'proto-European' warrior groups to intervene—periodically and decisively—in the geopolitics of ancient Near Eastern states. Ideas of this kind, laced with *Boy's Own* bravado, were offered to explain the collapse of palatial civilization throughout the Near East at the end of the Bronze Age. In his monumental *Struggle of the Nations*, Director General of Egyptian Antiquities Gaston Maspéro (1846-1916) drew particular attention to a scene carved on the walls of a New Kingdom temple at Abydos, in southern Egypt. It shows Ramesses the Great flanked by running bodyguards whose horned helmets and short swords identified them as *Shardana* (Sardinians) and, by the racial criteria of the day, as 'European' or 'Indo-Aryan'. The inability of a monarch to raise a native army, and his reliance upon foreign mercenaries, had been taken by European intellectuals since the Enlightenment as a defining characteristic and weakness of 'despotic' political systems. (The Ottoman Sultanate, which then controlled much of the Near East, was regarded as the prime exemplar by virtue of its dependence upon elite units of Mameluke and Janissary fighters.) Moreover, in Egyptian iconography the job of protecting the king's body usually falls to gods, not men, implying an almost superhuman status for these immigrant warriors. The monuments appeared to offer ancient foundations for what many Europeans felt was their pre-ordained role in the Near East: protectors and preservers of a civilized tradition, under threat from modern populations whose links to that tradition had long been severed, or had never existed at all.

Today the concept of civilization, reinvigorated after a brief post-colonial slumber, is undergoing a further transformation. 'Civilizations are dynamic; they rise and fall; they divide and merge. And, as any student of history knows, civilizations disappear and are buried in the sands of time.' The writer was Samuel Huntington, late Professor of the Science of Government at Harvard University. In 1993 he published an article entitled 'The Clash of Civilizations', which took issue with arguments presented by his former student, Francis Fukuyama. In a 1989 piece which later developed (as would Huntington's response) into a full-length book, Fukuyama had proposed that world history was entering a new phase, characterized by:

the end of mankind's ideological evolution and the univer-
salization of Western liberal democracy as the final form of
human government. This is not to say that there will no longer
be events to fill the pages of *Foreign Affairs*'s yearly summaries
of international relations, for the victory of liberalism has
occurred primarily in the realm of ideas or consciousness and
is as yet incomplete in the real or material world. But there
are powerful reasons for believing that it is the ideal that will
govern the material world *in the long run*.

Huntington disagreed. His response, which duly
appeared in the pages of *Foreign Affairs*, argued that
human societies—far from converging upon any
common form of organization—are in fact experiencing
a return to tribalism, and on a scale unprecedented in
history, a 'civilizational' scale. What Huntington meant
by civilization was made admirably clear in the opening
paragraphs of his essay:

A civilization is a cultural entity. Villages, regions, ethnic
groups, nationalities, religious groups, all have distinct
cultures at different levels of cultural heterogeneity. The
culture of a village in southern Italy may be different from
that of a village in northern Italy, but both will share in a
common Italian culture that distinguishes them from German
villages. European communities, in turn, will share cultural
features that distinguish them from Arab or Chinese communities. Arabs, Chinese and Westerners, however, are not part
of any broader cultural entity. They constitute civilizations.
A civilization is thus the highest cultural grouping of people
and the broadest level of cultural identity people have short of
that which distinguishes humans from other species. It is
defined both by common objective elements, such as language,

history, religion, customs, institutions, and by the subjective self-identification of people. People have levels of identity: a resident of Rome may define himself with varying degrees of intensity as a Roman, an Italian, a Catholic, a Christian, a European, a Westerner. The civilization to which he belongs is the broadest level of identification with which he intensely identifies. People can and do redefine their identities and, as a result, the composition and boundaries of civilizations change.

As Huntington developed his interpretation of current world affairs—the genocidal breakdown of former Yugoslavia, the proliferation of sophisticated weapons in non-Western states, and the formation of new economic blocs in East Asia—the concept of civilization began, for the umpteenth time in its turbulent history, to mutate, blending into the new political scenery, taking on new energy. Civilization, for Huntington, was rapidly becoming both cause and explanation for the uglier side of global politics, as well as the means to its resolution. The West, misguided in its old-fashioned and mono-lithic notion of civilization as a universal value, would now have to face up to the existence of 'civilizations', plural. In a vision that owes more than a little to the archaeological imagination, Huntington explains how the Cold War cast an ideological veil over deep and enduring fissures in the fabric of humanity, which—with the removal of the Iron Curtain—are now showing again on the surface of the globe. Humanity, he proph-esies, will be pulled apart along the bloodstained lines of old civilizations. Each of them is transnational in scope, is universal in outlook and ambition, and draws sustenance from firmly rooted—and mutually incompatible—beliefs about how people should live their lives, bury their dead, produce and consume goods, experience sexuality, and pursue spiritual fulfilment.

These arguments have provoked an outpouring of responses. Embraced by some political philosophers as revelatory wisdom, they are condemned by other commentators as monstrous abstractions: fuel to the flames of those very fundamentalisms they purport to oppose. In a scathing review for *The Nation* (October 2001) Edward Said, the late Professor of English and Comparative Literature at Columbia University, launched a frontal assault:

In fact, Huntington is an ideologist, someone who wants to make 'civilizations' and 'identities' into what they are not: shut-down, sealed-off entities that have been purged of the myriad currents and countercurrents that animate human history, and that over centuries have made it possible for that history not only to contain wars of religion and imperial conquest but also to be one of exchange, cross-fertilization and sharing. This far less visible history is ignored in the rush to highlight the ludicrously compressed and constricted warfare that 'the clash of civilizations' argues is the reality.

Remarkably, Huntington's thesis has as yet been little commented on by the rearguard of civilization studies— the archaeologists and anthropologists whose disciplines were first called into being as a means of establishing what civilizations are, how they first developed, and the manner in which they evolve. Huntington himself invited such commentary. In his expanded work on the clash of civilizations (subtitle: 'the remaking of world order'), he acknowledges and seeks to incorporate their contributions to the debate. The early history of civilizations that he sketches out is a history of isolates:

For more than three thousand years after civilizations first emerged, the contacts among them were, with some exceptions, either nonexistent or limited or intermittent and intense. The nature of these contacts is well expressed in the word historians use to describe them: 'encounters'. Civilizations were separated by time and space... Until 1500 the Andean and Mesoamerican civilizations had no contact with other civilizations or with each other. The early civilizations in the valleys of the Nile, Tigris-Euphrates, Indus and Yellow rivers also did not interact.

To illustrate the putative isolation of early civilizations, of no small importance for his larger arguments, Huntington borrows an image from Carroll Quigley's (1961) *The Evolution of Civilizations*. Resembling an inverted shrub, it portrays ancient civilizations as branching out from a common set of 'Neolithic Garden Cultures', carefully avoiding one another as they evolve, split, and mutate.

Part I of this book is a reply, by an archaeologist, to Huntington's claims about the lack of interaction between early civilizations. Its focus is the ancient Near East, which I take here to include both Egypt and Mesopotamia. But the points I make about the interconnectedness of prehistoric and ancient societies could be extended to all of the other regions mentioned by Huntington, and a considerable (if rather specialized) literature already exists to that effect. Some readers will by now be suspecting the presence in our midst of a straw man. Is it not obvious that Huntington, who never pretended to be an expert on the ancient world, has grossly overstated his case? Have not the connections between ancient Egypt, Mesopotamia, and their neighbours been recognized for well over a century?

My answer to this is that some straw men have a habit of resurrecting themselves, even after numerous attempts at incineration. Burning them is not a one-off exercise, but a 'moveable feast' that must be periodically repeated in order to remind us of what we already know, or have a tendency to forget. Most studies of 'early civilization' continue to focus upon a single region, or on a series of artificially isolated regions, with little attention to the relationships between them. By and large, we are still bound to a view of the ancient world as populated by 'Greeks', 'Egyptians', 'Mesopotamians', and so on, who are supposed to think and behave in distinctly 'Greek', 'Egyptian', 'Mesopotamian', etc., ways. The first part of this book questions the validity of such distinctions, arguing that cultural identities in the ancient Near East were the product of interaction and exchange, rather than isolation. But it also goes beyond these issues, to address the singular qualities that differentiate Egypt from Mesopotamia, and the persistence of those differences over thousands of years, despite the flow of influences and materials between them.

A Little Background

The study of Egypt and Mesopotamia does not begin on an equal footing. As one ancient historian observes, there has 'never been a "Babylonia-mania" in Western art, literature, architecture, or design to rival Egypt's hold on pre-modern Europe' (Lundquist 1995: 67). Certain features and memories of ancient Egyptian culture were known, celebrated, and imitated in the West long before the decipherment of the hieroglyphic script in the early nineteenth century, notably through the medium of biblical and Greco-Roman texts, as well as travellers' reports of the impressive stone monuments still visible on the Giza plateau and elsewhere in the valley of the Nile. The same sources also preserved a memory of the great empires of Mesopotamia, the land between the Tigris and Euphrates Rivers. The kingdoms of Assyria and Babylonia were recalled, if only through the eyes of those they subjugated. But by contrast, the earliest literate culture of the region—that of ancient Sumer, occupying today's southern Iraq—was completely unknown to European scholarship just a century ago. Its cities, temples, and scribal archives lay buried deep within the artificial mounds known as *tells*, formed by the accumulation of mud-brick architecture over millennia of human habitation.

Today we are aware that during the third millennium BC, which forms the chronological focus of this book, Egypt and Mesopotamia witnessed—more or less simultaneously—the emergence of dynastic polities on a scale then unprecedented in human history. Like their associated systems of writing, the earliest in the world, these polities took on strikingly different forms. The heartland of urban societies in Mesopotamia lay between the lower reaches of the Tigris and Euphrates Rivers, on the alluvial plains extending south of modern Baghdad to the marshy head of the Persian Gulf. By the end of the third millennium BC, written sources routinely refer to the southern part of this area as Sumer, a region made up of politically independent city-states in which a variety of languages (including Sumerian and Akkadian) were spoken, but whose inhabitants nevertheless recognized a common religious and cultural identity. By contrast, the 'Two Lands' of Upper and Lower Egypt—as hieroglyphic sources refer to the valley and delta of the Nile—constituted a single unified kingdom, held together by a sacred monarch whose territorial control extended from the First Cataract of the Nile at Elephantine (near modern Aswan) to the Mediterranean Sea.

Since Henri Frankfort wrote his *The Birth of Civilization in the Near East* (1951) (the last major comparative study of early Egypt and Mesopotamia) our understanding of these societies has increased exponentially. So too has the loss and destruction of ancient sites and artefacts through industrial dam construction, conflict, and looting. Dramatic increases in knowledge have

nevertheless taken place, notably in the field of prehistoric archaeology, providing a much fuller account of
the background to the emergence of the first dynastic
states in each region. And the spaces between and
adjacent to them have been gradually filled in by evidence
for societies of comparable scale and organizational
complexity, such as the remarkable kingdom of Ebla in
western Syria (whose capital, at Tell Mardikh, was
discovered by Italian scholars in the 1960s), and the
previously unsuspected Oxus (or 'Bactria-Margiana')
civilization of central Asia (uncovered by Russian
archaeologists in the 1970s). These new revelations, and
the dense web of connections which they reveal between
the societies of the ancient Near East, serve only to re-
inforce the interpretive challenge posed by 'the birth of
civilization':

For a comparison between Egypt and Mesopotamia discloses,
not only that writing, representational art, monumental
architecture, and a new kind of political coherence were
introduced in the two countries; it also reveals the striking
fact that the purpose of their writing, the contents of their
representations, the functions of their monumental buildings, and the structure of their new societies differed
completely. What we observe is not merely the establishment
of civilized life, but the emergence, concretely, of the distinctive 'forms' of Egyptian and Mesopotamian civilization.

(Frankfort 1951: 49)

PART I

THE CAULDRON OF CIVILIZATION

1

CAMOUFLAGED
BORROWINGS

> The history of civilization, from the point of view
> that concerns us, is the history of the circulation
> between societies of the various goods and achieve-
> ments of each. . . . Societies live by borrowing from
> each other, but they define themselves rather by the
> refusal of borrowing than by its acceptance.
>
> Marcel Mauss, *The Nation* (1920)

An Egyptian literary text dating to the end of the
Bronze Age (around 1100 BC) relates the journey
of Wenamun, an emissary of the Temple of Amon at
Thebes, to the port of Byblos, modern Jbeil, on the
coast of Lebanon. He is received by a local prince who
refuses to grant him the object of his mission: a consign-
ment of cedar wood, cut from the Lebanese mountains,
for the ceremonial river barge of the god Amon. An
affronted Wenamun reminds the prince that his royal
ancestors had always offered what is due to the supreme
god of Thebes: 'His is the sea, and his is Lebanon,
which you claim is yours.' The prince acknowledges

Amon's dominion over 'all the lands', but then goes on to remind Wenamun that 'technical skill'—the humanly learned skills of shipbuilding and maritime travel, for which Byblos was famed—has also spread 'as far as this place where I am', and with it the power conferred by mastery of the sea. He then proceeds to trade with Wenamun on his own, highly commercial, terms.

Marooned on the shores of Byblos, Wenamun was forced to learn a lesson that modern writers on the ancient world have often seen fit to ignore. We tend to portray ancient societies as existing rather like Shelley's famous description of Ozymandias, in splendid but desolate isolation. Regional specialists are not averse to claiming some elevated status for their particular area of expertise; and the layout of modern museums often militates against an understanding of the relationships *between* societies. Most seem to be planned on a principle of cultural quarantine, segregating the remains of once-connected civilizations into a series of artificial components: the isolated 'garden cultures' of Quigley's diagram. In consequence, we are easily startled by each new revelation of contact between peoples remote in time from ourselves. Like latter-day Wenamuns, caged within our particular world-views, we take for granted that isolation and stasis were the natural conditions of past societies, and that interaction between them was intermittent and exceptional—a series of 'encounters', as Huntington puts it.

In reflecting upon these assumptions, let us return to the narrow coastal strip of the northern Levant (modern-day Syria and Lebanon) and its mountainous hinterland, raised high above the Mediterranean by the Great Rift Valley on its passage from the lakes of East Africa to the foothills of southern Turkey. In the vicinity of these mountains, with their lofty stands of cedar and juniper, the political imaginations and economic interests of the world's first states converged. Hereabouts, and most probably in the Amanus Mountains of northern Syria, lay the inspiration for the 'Cedar Forest' of Mesopotamian literature, where Gilgamesh—the exemplary king of Mesopotamian legend—slew the monstrous guardian of the woods and, together with his bounty of fine timber, made the long return journey down the Euphrates to the city of Uruk, near the head of the Persian Gulf. A short way to the south, along the Lebanon and Anti-Lebanon ranges, was located a domain of the goddess Ba'alat Gebal, also recognized as the Egyptian Hathor in her guise of the 'Lady of the Mountain'. Many centuries before Wenamun, emissaries of the Egyptian court docked at the harbour of Byblos to worship at her sanctuary and obtain a variety of exotic trade goods. Most important among them were timber, and also the resins of coniferous trees, which were applied to the bodies of the elite dead during their preparation for the tomb.

Today the denuded slopes of the Syrian and Lebanese mountains stand as testimony to millennia of exploitation, their deeper scars reaching back to a time when the products of the Canaanite coast fed the demands of distant gods on the Nile and the Euphrates. But how typical or frequent were such long-distance transfers of goods and knowledge between the ancient states of the Near East? What role did they play in the ancient economy? Despite their impressive scale and sophistication, there is no written evidence that the kingdom of Egypt and the city-states of Mesopotamia were directly aware of one another during their first thousand years of existence, which correspond roughly to the third millennium BC. The horizons of the known world, when traced from the official records of either region, appear more limited: ships that passed in the night. Can we then conclude, with Huntington, that the flow of interaction between them was negligible and inconsequential?

False Horizons

Ancient Egyptian written sources identify a variety of foreign territories and peoples beyond, and subservient to, the 'Two Lands'; a term which referred both to the political frontiers of the kingdom and to the cultivable parts of the Nile valley and delta. Among them we find the pastoral tribes of the Eastern and Western Deserts of Egypt; the people of Nubia, beyond the First Cataract of the Nile; the towns of the Levantine coast, among which Byblos was accorded special status as an appendage of the royal court and a domain of Hathor; the Sinai Desert, with its mines of turquoise and copper; and *Punt*, a land of natural wonders along the southern

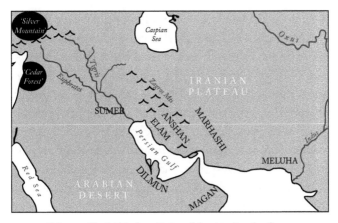

Map 2. Probable locations of foreign lands, from Mesopotamian sources

reaches of the Red Sea, and a supplier of aromatic incense for the purification of temples and tombs.

Mesopotamian royal inscriptions, from the late third millennium BC onwards, routinely assert the conquest of 'all the peoples and mountain lands from across the Lower Sea to the Upper Sea', referring respectively to the waters of the Persian Gulf and the Caspian Sea, or possibly Lake Urmia to the west. The northerly limits of the cosmos were also fixed by the 'Cedar Forest' and 'Silver Mountain', places of heroic battles and supernatural encounters beyond the reach of ordinary mortals. The main maritime arena lay to the south, within and beyond the 'Lower Sea'. The name *Dilmun*, already mentioned in cuneiform documents of the late fourth millennium BC, refers at various times to the islands of

Bahrain and Tarut, and to the adjoining Arabian littoral of the central Gulf; and by the end of the third millennium, more distant locations had been added: *Magan* (the Gulf of Oman, rich in copper ores) and *Meluha* (most probably the coastal sweep between Makran and the mouths of the Indus, identified as a supplier of exotic goods such as ivory, lapis lazuli, carnelian, gold, and fine woods). The kingdom of *Elam*, with its lowland capital at Susa in south-west Iran, and the more distant territories of *Anshan* and *Marhashi* in the Iranian highlands to the east are acknowledged in Mesopotamian sources as political equals and rivals to the cities of the Sumerian plain.

The scope of these geographical designations was not rigidly fixed, changing with experience and perhaps also with the contexts in which they were used. At times the 'Upper Sea' seems to refer to the Mediterranean, rather than Caspian, as in a victory inscription of Sargon of Akkad (*c.*2300 BC) which places it near the Silver Mountain (most likely the Bolkardağ mines on the slopes of the Taurus in southern Turkey, overlooking the Cilician Gates). From the internal perspective of Mesopotamian royal rhetoric, the distinction between these two bodies of water—Mediterranean and Caspian—need not always have been significant. The political imagination has a timeless habit of polarizing space into 'Upper/Lower', 'Inner/Outer', 'East/West'. But there are other reasons why toponyms of this kind should not be taken as an accurate guide to the extent of cross-cultural interaction in the ancient Near East. These reasons become clearer when we consider the principal functions and distribution of the early writing systems from which they derive.

In Egypt the ceremonial hieroglyphic script and its cursive variant, known as hieratic, appeared together around 3300 BC. Cuneiform writing was invented around the same time in Sumer, where its use was initially restricted to the notation of economic accounts. The signs of the cuneiform script, impressed with a reed stylus onto tablets of damp clay, were initially pictorial in character, but over a period of centuries they were reduced to more abstract forms for speed and ease of execution. By contrast, the hieroglyphic script of Egypt never lost its pictorial character. It was carved on a wide variety of display media, whose overwhelmingly royal functions reflect the restricted social context of the script's invention. The more informal hieratic script was used in Egypt for administration and was executed with ink on papyrus, which rarely survives from such early periods, or on the surface of ceramic containers. Inscribed Egyptian objects occasionally made their way abroad as a result of trading ventures and diplomatic activity. By the beginning of the second millennium BC small numbers were carried as far as the island of Crete where distinct systems of pictorial and linear (non-pictorial) writing— probably unrelated to those of Egypt, but with possible antecedents on the Levantine coast—subsequently developed. Regular use of the Egyptian writing system, however, remained firmly confined to the territory of the Egyptian state, including its garrisons in Nubia, and its oasis colonies in the Eastern Sahara where clay tablets were sometimes employed as a convenient substitute for papyrus.

Of the two systems, Egyptian and Mesopotamian, cuneiform was by far the more promiscuous. By 3000 BC its use in Sumer had stimulated the development of a closely related writing system to the east, in the lowland towns of neighbouring Khuzestan (south-west Iran), and from there an independent network of literate communities—smaller in scale than those of Sumer—extended into highland Iran and beyond to the vicinity of modern-day Tehran. This latter script, known as 'Proto-Elamite', is still far from being deciphered, but its early uses seem to have been largely restricted to administration and accounting. By no later than 2400 BC cuneiform writing was also employed in palatial centres on the Middle Euphrates (Mari) and beyond the Syrian steppe (Ebla), where it was used to record languages of the Semitic family (to which Sumerian, the earliest written language of southern Mesopotamia, is an outsider). The Harappan civilization of the Indus valley—a contemporary of Old Kingdom Egypt and Early Dynastic Mesopotamia—also developed its own script. Unrelated to cuneiform and known largely from engravings on stone commodity seals, the early Indus script remains undeciphered.

This may seem an impressive roster of script-using societies clustered within a relatively small portion of the globe. (The term 'literate societies' is not ideal, since the restricted groups that used scripts were, in Benedict

Anderson's words, 'tiny literate reefs on top of vast illiterate oceans'.) Yet, with the exception of the palatial archive at Ebla, the surviving administrative records of early states provide only vague and sporadic clues regarding their relationships with societies beyond their political frontiers. Nor do they reveal much about the manner in which technological skills—including the skill of writing itself—were learned and transmitted within and between societies. Most of the economic archives which have been studied are narrowly concerned with the internal affairs of urban institutions, rather than with long-distance trade.

Both in Egypt and in Mesopotamia, official representations of the outside world are more commonly preserved on royal monuments erected in temples, tombs, and palaces. Their messages were directed towards the inner elite and to the gods, and their cartography is cosmic rather than secular in nature. Contact and exchange with foreign lands played an integral role in such representations, but it was a role defined first and foremost by ritual and political concerns. They tell us much about the internal workings and needs of Egyptian and Sumerian society, and especially their institutions of sacral kingship, which I explore in Chapter 8. But they are of limited value in reconstructing the true extent of contact between ancient societies. Given these limitations to our written evidence for cross-cultural interaction, it is necessary to stress the social and ecological imperatives that compelled early states into constant interaction with the outside world.

Imperatives to Interaction

The agrarian economies of Egypt and Sumer were entirely dependent on the fertile alluvial soils deposited by their major river systems, which passed through otherwise arid regions that experienced negligible rainfall. The flood regimes of the Tigris and Euphrates were much less favourable to irrigation agriculture than that of the Nile, rising with the spring harvest rather than in the autumn sowing season, when water is most in demand. Accordingly they required a higher investment of labour to maintain artificial water channels and dykes, and to prevent the build-up of toxic salts in the soil. Under stable climatic conditions, both regions nevertheless enjoyed rich annual yields of cereals, legumes, and tree crops, supplemented by abundant wild resources. Their respective locations on major floodplains, however, also rendered the polities of Egypt and Mesopotamia dependent on outside sources for a wide variety of raw materials. Metals, hard stones, and high quality timber had to be regularly obtained from remote regions, often located hundreds or even thousands of kilometres away, and inhabited by non-literate societies whose histories must be reconstructed primarily from their surviving material cultures.

With their limited military capacity, Old Kingdom Egypt and the Early Dynastic city-states of Sumer resorted only sporadically to direct force as a means of directing the activities of smaller groups on their margins, which developed their own forms of resistance to outside interference (discussed in Chapter 6). Formal empires were not a feature of this period, although from the closing centuries of the third millennium BC the trend of development in both regions was towards their formation on ever-larger scales. The importance of the Nile, the Tigris, and the Euphrates therefore lay as much in their role as arteries of trade and communication between the urban and non-urban worlds, as in the agricultural surpluses afforded by their annual floods.

In assessing the significance of such long-distance transfers it is misleading to refer to metals, timber, coloured stone, tree resins, and aromatics as 'exotica' or 'luxuries'. This diminishes their importance, implying that they were little more than 'optional extras' for elite groups whose power over their subordinates was otherwise assured. Such views may have been tenable in the late nineteenth and early twentieth centuries. At that time it was widely believed that, in dry climates, the political structures of 'despotic' states were a direct outgrowth of their dominant mode of farming, using irrigation channels to water otherwise arid and infertile lands. Political historians such as Karl Wittfogel, adapting Marx's definition of an 'Asiatic mode of production', argued strongly that centralized bureaucracy—and the hierarchies it supported—were grounded in the managerial requirements and inherent inequities of large-scale irrigation farming. But it has since become apparent that irrigation arrangements and the direct organization of arable land feature little in early administrative records from Egypt and Mesopotamia. Most farming took place in a fairly decentralized manner, making use of natural flood basins and well-drained levee soils formed by the annual inundations of their respective river systems, a view supported by detailed archaeological surveys in both regions. It has also become clear that small-scale irrigation networks—and the customary systems of cooperation and conflict-resolution required to manage them—had a deep prehistory extending back to pre-urban times (the earliest, excavated in central Iraq and western Iran, date to the sixth millennium BC), and continued to operate long after the emergence (and subsequent collapse) of centralized political systems. Recent fieldwork in northern Syria (notably at the site of Tell Brak, on a tributary of the Khabur River) further demonstrates a precocious growth of urban settlement and bureaucracy around 4000 BC, in a region where rainfall was sufficient to support agriculture without recourse to irrigation.

As Jonathan Friedman and Kajsa Eckholm (1979) argued some decades ago, 'to insist, as is usually done, that the evolution of high cultures is based on the agricultural surplus of intensive irrigation is to systematically avoid the problem that surplus grain cannot be locally transformed into bronze, cloth, palaces (of imported stone), fine jewellery and weapons—hallmarks of the great civilization.' It was precisely through the acquisition and strategic deployment of these 'outside' resources—as markers of distinction, as forms of currency, and as signs of sacred power—that dynastic elites maintained their special relationship to the society of the gods, which in turn legitimated the hierarchical structures of human societies. Here we encounter a paradox to which I will return numerous times throughout this book: it was through contact with their gods that the societies of Egypt and Mesopotamia expressed their uniqueness, their distinct attachments to land, locality, origins, and place. Yet the earthly bodies of the Egyptian and Mesopotamian gods were ritually manufactured, nourished, and cared for in similar ways, using similar materials that could not be found locally in either area. In seeking to understand the roots of cultural difference—the distinctive 'forms' of Egyptian and Mesopotamian civilization—we are therefore drawn inexorably into a world of mixtures and borrowings. The outer contours of that world can be traced, in a preliminary fashion, through the lens of a single medium: the iridescent blue stone known as lapis lazuli.

2

ON THE TRAIL OF
BLUE-HAIRED GODS

Yet there are sufficient reflections of *Gilgamesh* and other Near Eastern epics, tales, and literary motifs within Homeric epic to make quite clear that Near Eastern epic was probably quite familiar in the Aegean area, and not only at the time (roughly around 700 BC) when the Homeric epics themselves are believed to have been composed.

Susan Sherratt, 'Archaeological Contexts' (2005)

Among the most remarkable archaeological discoveries of recent years are the gold casings of two human figures, respectively 60 and 30 centimetres tall, found within a mud-brick building in northern Egypt, and dated to around 3200 BC. Metalwork of any kind is rarely preserved from such remote periods. Most was melted down and recycled in antiquity. The statue coverings from Tell el-Farkha, a cluster of low mounds in the Nile Delta, are a startling exception to this rule of preservation. Carefully reconstructed, they now lie in state in the Cairo Museum. Here and there remain gaps in the reconstruction, chinks in their armour through which passes light refracted from their glass cases, robbing them of the illusion of solidity. Also on display are the tiny gold rivets that once pierced these metallic skins, pinning them to wooden cores which have long since decayed; and a bead necklace upon which was strung a large disc of deep red carnelian.

With their mask-like faces, tall penis sheaths, and strangely elongated fingers, the statue coverings are a disconcerting sight for visitors attuned to the bodily aesthetics of later Egyptian art, who may feel that they have accidentally intruded upon a different, more alien cultural realm. Yet in one respect, they stand clearly and firmly at the beginning of a long-lived tradition of royal representation. All is in the eyes and eyebrows, cut away to receive the deep blue inlays of lapis lazuli which are still visible around the smaller of the two faces. Many centuries later the same iridescent stone, flecked with golden pyrite, still framed the eyes of Tutankhamun's funerary mask (1327 BC), and enclosed the protective eye of the god Horus on bracelets around the mummified arms of Shoshenq II (890 BC) in his tomb at Tanis, then the gateway to the Mediterranean world from which Wenamun departed on his journey to Byblos.

On royal and divine statuary, Egyptian artisans often combined lapis with turquoise mined from the Sinai Desert, where Old Kingdom rock carvings proclaim the king's control over the land and its resources. Blue glass and the silica compound known as faience were most likely invented to imitate the aesthetic properties of these coveted stones, and to disseminate their magical properties beyond the inner elite. A common Mesopotamian term for 'glass' is 'stone of the kiln' (as opposed to 'the mountain'), while Egyptian sources refer to it as 'stone of the kind that flows'. By the middle of the second millennium BC, local manufacture of these vitreous materials—rendered from common quartz sand with tiny admixtures of precious minerals—had spread westwards towards the Aegean, where real lapis beads were found by Heinrich Schliemann over a century ago, ornamenting the bodies of warrior-kings buried in the Shaft Graves of Mycenae (*c.*1600 BC).

In Mesopotamia, as in Egypt, the sacred aesthetics of blue hair is widely in evidence. Thin bands of lapis form the eyes and eyebrows of serene statuettes from the Early Bronze Age palace at Mari (*c.*2500 BC). And the Royal Tombs of Ur, of broadly the same date, supply evidence of collective funerary rites in which entire royal households—warriors, musicians, and female mourners bedecked in elaborate headdresses of gold and lapis—confronted their shared death in a pageant of solar yellow and night-time blue, their bodies anointed with liquids poured from conch shells, drawn from the Indian Ocean. An Egyptian ritual incantation inscribed within the pyramid of Unas around 2350 BC empowers the dead king to 'cultivate lapis lazuli' just as he makes acacia grow along the Nile, and binds together the cords of plants whose knotted stems embody the unity of the Two Lands. And in the epics of the Sumerian kings,

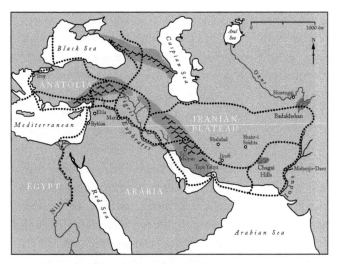

Map 3. The lapis lazuli route, from Afghanistan to
the Mediterranean, *c.*2500 BC

composed around the same time, it is the desire for blue
stone to furnish the temple of the goddess Inanna that
drives the rulers of Uruk into competition with the lord
of *Aratta*: a mythical city beyond the eastern mountains,
whose inhabitants are said to 'cut the pure lapis lazuli
from its block' (Chapter 5). In Egyptian cosmology, the
visual properties of this blue stone are closely linked to
concepts of life force, organic growth, and regeneration;
while in Mesopotamian literature, as the archaeologist
Dan Potts (1997) points out, 'lapis-like' was a standard
metaphor for great riches, 'a synonym for all things
bright and splendid, especially the beard or other
features of heroes and deities'.

Deeply woven into the sacred and political landscapes of the Nile Valley and the Mesopotamian alluvium, lapis lazuli (like gold) was nevertheless exotic to both. The nearest sources of lapis lay far to the east, above the winding river valleys of Badakhshan in northern Afghanistan, and in the rugged folds of the Chagai Hills, in western Pakistan. To arrive in either region over land this material first had to circumvent the great wastes of the Iranian Plateau—the Dasht-e Kavir and the Dasht-e Lut—penetrating the Zagros Mountains through one of a small number of seasonal passes that opened onto the fertile alluvial plains of the Tigris. From there it was transported by donkey caravan or wheeled carts directly across the plains of northern Iraq, or up the Euphrates and then west to the Mediterranean coast, passing along the Syrian Saddle; a grassy corridor between the mountains and the desert, traversing the hundred or so miles from north-west Mesopotamia to the Gulf of Iskenderun (Greek Alexandretta).

The overland passages through highland Iran were difficult, becoming choked with snow in the winter months. During the course of the third millennium BC they seem to have been gradually superseded by maritime commerce in the Arabian Sea, which provided faster and more economic links for traders supplying Central Asian goods to the city-states of Sumer. Ships carrying precious minerals (including lapis) and a variety of other commodities set sail from anchorage points along the arid Makran coastline of southern

Pakistan, which was isolated from the worst effects of the summer monsoon, entering the Persian Gulf via the Straits of Hormuz. The port today called Bandar Abbas, sitting directly astride the Straits, may have provided a second major maritime outlet with ready access to the Iranian Plateau via the Halil River, where an important urban settlement—and epicentre of a far-flung trade in ornate stone vessels, the distribution of which reaches from the Indus to the eastern Mediterranean—has been located at the site of Jiroft, in southern Iran.

Like the Silk and Spice Roads of later antiquity, the Bronze Age lapis routes were more than just conduits for material resources. They were also the channels along which meanings and values spread between otherwise disparate groups, crossing the four thousand miles of mountain, desert, and plain that separate the mines of Badakhshan from the mouth of the Nile. As the largest consumers of metals and minerals in the region, the city-states of lowland Mesopotamia, whose populations can only be crudely estimated in tens of thousands, played a dominant role in this process of transmission. Tastes cultivated there influenced patterns of consumption far beyond the Sumerian plain. Among the cuneiform archives at Ebla, on the edge of the Syrian steppe, was found a manual listing more than fifty different varieties of lapis lazuli, known by both their local and Sumerian names. A rich cache of personal ornaments, recovered from the palace at Mari, further demonstrates the strong influence of Sumerian fashions at a key transit point between Mesopotamia, the Anatolian highlands, and the Syrian coast. And specific parallels for complex styles of jewellery, found in abundance in the Royal Tombs of Ur, can be documented across a truly vast area, extending from the city of Mohenjo-daro on the floodplain of the Indus to the fortified citadel of Hissarlik, the site of Homer's Troy, overlooking the Aegean Sea (Chapter 6). The classical historian Robert Drew Griffith (2005) notes how Homer's deities, and the heroes under their protection, are distinguished from ordinary mortals by their blue hair, eyebrows, and lashes, a legacy, perhaps, from the gods of the ancient Near East?

Following the trail of the blue-haired gods, we are confronted by more questions than answers. Why should an apparently arbitrary equation between the experience of the sacred and the aesthetic qualities of a particular coloured stone be replicated across such enormous distances, and such varied cultural settings? How did lapis attain a value and exclusivity that cut across the boundaries of visual style and representation, which so clearly distinguish the products of Egyptian craft workers from those of Mesopotamia? By what processes did such distinct cosmologies as those of Egypt and Sumer come to share a common material of construction, exotic to both? As will become apparent, we are not dealing here with an isolated case of diffusion, but rather with a key that unlocks a larger realm of camouflaged borrowings.

3

NEOLITHIC WORLDS

It was in Neolithic times that man's mastery of the great arts of civilization—of pottery, weaving, agriculture and the domestication of animals— became firmly established...Each of these techniques assumes centuries of active and methodical observation.

Claude Lévi-Strauss, *The Savage Mind* (1966)

Like honey and imported cedar resin, which Sumerian kings mixed into the mortar of mud-bricks to bring blessings upon a new temple, lapis lazuli may be usefully characterized as a 'sticky' material. Not quite, perhaps, in the literal sense of a physical adhesive, but rather in the sense of a social attractor; a material towards which beneficial acts and forces gravitate. Blue, especially when applied to the staring eyes of votive statues, was the colour of supplication, inviting offerings and good fortune, and small tablets of lapis lazuli have been found within the foundations of Early Dynastic temples at Mari and Uruk, where they were carefully placed during rituals that marked the various stages of building a sacred dwelling. Above all, lapis was an attractor for other dazzling materials, especially gold and tin (the crucial additive to copper in making bronze), sources of which clustered along the river valleys between Kandahar and Kabul, where lapis cobbles could also be found (Chapter 6). But the close association between lapis and other exotic materials can be traced back far beyond the Bronze Age.

At the site of Tepe Gawra, on a tributary of the Tigris River with seasonal access to the Iranian highlands, a grave dating to around 4000 BC was found to contain lapis eye-shaped ornaments (perhaps from a statue), around five hundred lapis beads, and a hair ornament composed of lapis, turquoise, and gold. Suggestive traces of blue pigment were also noted around the head and upper body of the individual interred there. The other contents of this burial form a remarkably complete inventory of the exotic highland materials then already in circulation on the Mesopotamian plains, among them some hundreds of turquoise beads, gold body ornaments, electrum beads (made from an alloy of gold and silver), and two blades worked from obsidian—a dark volcanic stone whose sources lie in the remote uplands of central and eastern Turkey. In Egypt lapis beads first appear in prehistoric burials of the fourth millennium BC, some centuries older than the Tell el-Farkha statues. Here again the blue stone did not travel alone, but was accompanied by shells and other coloured ornaments made from minerals extracted along the desert margins of the Red Sea coast.

The 'Fertile Crescent': Crossroads of Africa and Eurasia

Such long-range movements of precious highland minerals are, in fact, a much older feature of life in the Near East than these limited examples suggest. Lapis lazuli was a relatively late arrival on the scene, making its first documented appearance in lowland Mesopotamia during the sixth millennium BC. Thousands of years earlier, the first farmers of the 'Fertile Crescent'—the bridge between Africa and Eurasia, and the setting for the earliest domestication of plants and animals—were already accomplished traders in obsidian, marine shells; ornaments of horn, tooth, and bone; and a host of organic commodities.

In a very practical sense, the vertical movement of resources from uplands to lowlands was integral to the transition from hunter-gatherer to early farming economies, the hallmark of the Neolithic period. To evolve into fully domestic strains, the earliest cultivated cereals (wheat and barley) and managed herd animals (sheep and goat) had to be genetically isolated from their wild progenitors, a process which involved downward transplantation—by human, rather than natural, agency—from their native habitats on the slopes of hills and mountains (where the first experiments in domestication took place) to the seasonally watered soils of oases, lake margins, and river fans, where farming became fully established. Such restricted lowland environments—rich in mud and clay, but poor in most other forms of mineral life—are well exemplified by the spring of 'Ain es-Sultan (Jericho), on the outskirts of the Jordan valley in modern-day Palestine. There, in the shadow of the Judean Mountains, Neolithic settlement around 9000 BC produced a town of some three hectares, overlooked by a monumental stone tower and terracing systems, defending its mud-brick streets and houses against the seasonal incursion of floodwaters.

Within centuries, similar lowland niches had been colonized by farming groups around virtually the whole of the Fertile Crescent, as far east as the arid plain of Deh Luran in south-west Iran, watered by streams descending from the foothills of the Zagros Mountains. The growth of permanent settlements, with their vernacular forms of mud-brick architecture, gave rise to a distinctive landscape of *tells*: artificial mounds built up over centuries of sedentary occupation. Some thousands of these man-made hills—vestiges of a mode of habitation now all-but-extinct—can be seen today across a large swathe of Eurasia, from the Balkans to western India. The landscape of prehistoric and Bronze Age tells also extends tentatively onto the African landmass, colonizing sandy promontories that project above the floodplain of the Nile Delta.

The Neolithic communities of the Near East, which took form after the end of the last Ice Age (*c.*12,000 BC), were the forerunners of urban societies not just in their agricultural achievements, but in a whole variety of social and technological innovations. As early as 8500 BC, small groups of colonists were making the crossing from the Turkish or Syrian coast to eastern Cyprus in sail-less boats, laden with large fauna (cattle, pig, sheep, goat, and fallow deer). The same groups also carried cereal crops and obsidian from sources in the highlands of central Turkey, traces of which have been unearthed in the island settlements they founded. On the opposite side of the Fertile Crescent there are tantalizing indications that, by the late sixth millennium BC, simple sail-powered craft may already have been plying the route from southern Mesopotamia to the Gulf of Oman, where the coastal waters teemed with fish and edible molluscs.

While the maritime crossing to Cyprus may have been the work of groups already firmly committed to a farming lifestyle, the development of sailing technology probably owes more to populations of hunter-gatherer-fishers who continued to inhabit coastlands and marshy river mouths opening onto the Arabian Sea, long after groups further inland had adopted an agricultural mode of existence. Hunters and foragers, contemporaries of the earliest farmers, also appear to be at least partly responsible for the earliest known examples of monumental sculpture in the Near East (c.9000 BC), which can no longer be regarded as a distinct achievement of urban societies. This is dramatically exemplified at Göbekli Tepe, a site raised high above the plains of southern Turkey, where ceremonial centres—populated by gigantic stone images of ferocious animals, some fully sculpted and others carved in relief onto T-shaped pillars over 3 metres high—stand guard between the Mesopotamian lowlands and the hilly passes leading into the Taurus Mountains. Unlike the free-standing megaliths of western Europe, constructed some six millennia later, the standing stones of Göbekli Tepe are lodged within the walls of circular or apsidal buildings. Once regarded, like monumental architecture, as an urban innovation, the systematic extraction of milk from herd animals and its processing into dairy products can now also be traced back to a much earlier period (the seventh millennium BC), most clearly among the early cattle-keepers of western Turkey. Rather than a uniform progression of technological stages, followed simultaneously by communities across the Near East, these various innovations took place in specific social and environmental contexts, only then spreading along expanding lines of contact and exchange.

Between Continents: Egypt on the Prehistoric Fringe

Social forms and material forms interpenetrate. Among Neolithic societies, the distribution of materials used as personal ornamentation, such as coloured stones and marine shells, maps out recognizable 'circuits' or 'networks' of exchange, the shifting contours of which can be traced over millennia of prehistoric interaction. Long before the epics of Gilgamesh were committed to writing, the inhabitants of the Fertile Crescent no doubt told stories of heroic journeys to distant mountains in search of jealously guarded bounty. Some flavour of these lost worlds

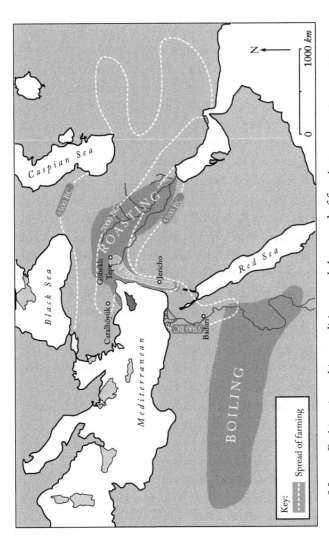

Map 4. Prehistoric cooking traditions, and the spread of farming, c.10,000 to 5000 BC

of the imagination is preserved in the complex traces of Neolithic art and ritual, which again fall into recognizable regional styles, smaller than—and interlaced by—the more extensive networks of cross-regional trade.

To the modern eye, the excavated remnants of Neolithic villages (c.9000–7000 BC) from the plains of central Turkey to the foothills of the Zagros often resemble complex art installations: elaborate microcosms, where the dwelling spaces of the living merge with the remains of the dead and with the body-parts of wild animals, brought into and displayed within domestic houses: a 'cultural domestication' which, as Ian Hodder (1990) points out, often foreshadowed biological domestication. From the Jordan Valley to the Middle Euphrates, we also find the dismembered skulls of the ancestral dead—carefully curated, and revivified with plaster and paint—stored beneath house-floors and village squares. Some were ornamented with cowrie shell eyes, or anointed with exotic pigments; tangible evidence of their links to faraway places and people. Later, when painted pottery was introduced (c.7000–5000 BC) these ancestral rites were abandoned or transformed in favour of new ceremonies of hospitality and kinship. Again the richly painted ceramics (and no doubt the styles of decorated basketry, which they so carefully emulate) fall into clear zones of distribution: shared worlds of domestic ritual, linking villages hundreds of kilometres apart on the Mesopotamian lowlands.

The Neolithic societies of Egypt and Sudan (c.6000–4000 BC) borrowed selectively from their neighbours to the east, cultivating not just new plants and animals, but also a distinctive regional identity which is evident in every facet of their material remains, and which I go on to describe in the section that follows. But Egypt also lay on the cusp of a major divergence in prehistoric societies, which long precedes the origins of farming. As Randi Haaland (2007) observes, this divergence is most clearly evident in modes of food preparation and consumption, initially applied to wild plant and animal species. Assemblages of ceramic cooking vessels, dating back to around 9000 BC, have been found across much of what is now the Sahara Desert, including the Sudanese (but not Egyptian) part of the Nile Valley. Between around ten and six thousand years ago much of this region—from the Red Sea to the Atlantic coast—was savannah, occupied by widely dispersed communities of hunters, fishers, and foragers who led relatively sedentary lives, concentrated around shallow lakes and surrounding wetlands. These early Saharan ceramics are among the world's oldest, rivalled only by the early pottery traditions of eastern Asia. They were decorated with impressed designs, executed with fish-spines, probably to imitate the appearance of netting. In the Fertile Crescent of south-west Asia, by contrast, pottery production was rare or non-existent for some thousands of years after the beginnings of agriculture, making its first widespread appearance (in both plain and painted forms) only around 7000 BC.

As Dorian Fuller and Michael Rowlands (2010) have noted, this broad regional contrast is best explained by the different processing techniques used to release nutrients and remove toxins from wild plant resources, techniques which seem to have been replicated over extremely large areas. Across much of northern Africa the early presence of ceramics implies forms of cuisine in which locally abundant cereals (millet and sorghum) were transformed into nutritious foods (porridge and beer) by boiling, just as fish and other meats were cooked mainly by stewing in sealed containers. In western Asia, where pottery was initially absent, a contrasting emphasis can be found upon the grinding of wild plants (including native wheat and barley) into flour and their subsequent baking to make flat breads (ancestors of the pita and chapatti), which went together with the open-air roasting of meats. At the site of Ohalo, by the shores of the Sea of Galilee in northern Israel, this grinding-and-roasting tradition can be traced back to 20,000 BC, some ten millennia before the onset of farming. Neolithic societies along the Egyptian Nile may initially have adopted elements of both culinary traditions. But there is no doubt that by 4000 BC, when evidence for larger settlements begins to emerge, Egypt had become fully incorporated into what David Edwards (2003) terms the 'bread-eating world' of western Asia.

The implications of this regional contrast between cooking traditions based on boiling and roasting extends far beyond matters of diet. Bread came to play a central role in the dynastic societies of Egypt and Mesopotamia, both as a staple food and as a component of sacrificial offerings presented to gods and ancestors (further discussed in Chapter 7). In both areas the baking of processed cereals and the roasting of meat were central elements of religious feasting. Fuller and Rowlands observe how these particular modes of culinary devotion can be seen to derive from a common cultural reservoir that was exclusive to neither the Nile nor the Euphrates, but was instead the outcome of (pre)historical connections between them, connections which also extended to neighbouring societies across much of western Eurasia. While allowing for such underlying commonalities, however, it is important to recognize significant differences in the forms of Neolithic society that developed in the Nile Valley and south-west Asia, and to acknowledge the close affinities that also existed between Egypt and her African neighbours to the south.

Body Cultures: The Nile and North-East Africa

Throughout the Egyptian Nile Valley and southwards to the convergence of the Blue and White Niles in central Sudan, Neolithic cemeteries of a broadly similar kind have been excavated along the arid margins of the floodplain, where lack of moisture guards against the decomposition of their contents. Among the many hundreds of known Neolithic burials—of men, women, and children—it is difficult to find even one in which the corpse has not been carefully wrapped and adorned with the customary equipment for social life: clothing made from the hides of cattle and other animals, a rich toolkit of cosmetic instruments including stone palettes on which pigments (collected from the Eastern Desert) were ground to make body paint, a bewildering variety of small vessels for food and medicine, and exuberant beadwork comprising such exotic elements as shells, jasper, and carnelian from the Red Sea littoral, and turquoise brought from the Sinai Desert. By 3500 BC experiments were underway to further extend the symbolic potential of the body in death through artificial preservation with resin-soaked bindings (the beginnings of mummification), but also through the post-mortem dismemberment and separate burial of various body-parts. Combs, pins, bangles, cosmetic palettes, and ceramic vessels—the conventional tools of self-presentation—were also newly elaborated at this time with images of wild animals, plants, and other natural features: miniature landscapes distributed over a shifting topography of human forms. Five centuries later (*c.*3000 BC) these same object types had become conventional—but, by this time, highly restricted—media of royal display.

Here emerges an important and long-lived contrast between the prehistoric communities of the Nile Valley and south-west Asia, one still clearly discernible centuries later in the literature and monuments of dynastic Egypt and Mesopotamia (Chapter 8). At a broad level of generality it can be observed that Neolithic communities in western Asia recognized strong symbolic and material affinities between the substance of human bodies and the substance of houses. Houses contained the activities of the living, but were also partly composed of the bodily remains of the dead, which were physically incorporated into their clay fittings and furnishings. De-fleshed bones, when not stored and archived in special charnel houses, were built into domestic spaces; and the disarticulated skulls of certain individuals, as mentioned earlier, were accorded special treatment, coated with the same plaster and paint used to regenerate the ageing surfaces of domestic buildings. Local funerary traditions varied, but a broad concern with the material fabric of the house as a point of communion with the dead can nevertheless be identified across this entire region, from central Turkey to the Zagros piedmont. The Neolithic societies of the Nile Valley were different. Certainly they exploited a wide array of materials such as reeds, acacia, and alluvial mud in the construction of domestic dwellings. Yet the household seems not to have played an equivalent role as focal setting and substance for the ritual life of the group. To a far greater extent, it was through and upon the structure of the *body itself*—its skin and hair; its diverse contents; its emissions and cavities; its passage between life and death—that the community inscribed its presence in the landscape, and celebrated the enduring vitality of its institutions.

In drawing such a broad regional contrast between the Neolithic cultures of the Nile Valley and southwest Asia—with their respective emphasis upon the elaboration of 'body' and 'house' as metaphors and materials of social attachment—it is important to recall that the differences were not born of isolation, but through a long process of exchange and interaction. None of the domestic plant and animal species on which the dynastic economy of Egypt was based were indigenous to the African continent. Wheat, barley, and flax for linen—often wrongly considered 'immemorial' features of the Egyptian landscape on the basis of later tomb depictions—all had to be introduced from outside, and were present only after about 4500 BC. The native fauna of North Africa included Barbary sheep and wild cattle, which may have been subject to local forms of herd-management as early as 9000 BC. But none of these experiments seem to have resulted in any lasting interdependence between humans and the species involved.

Only around 6000 BC were fully domesticated varieties of sheep and goat introduced to Egypt from the Fertile Crescent of south-west Asia. On current evidence, the main route of transfer may well have been a maritime one, arriving at a point on the Red Sea coast and reaching the Nile Valley via a network of seasonal river-channels (or *wadis*). Today these channels are thoroughly dried out, but they once supported a range of fauna and flora, richly depicted in the rock art of Egypt's Eastern Desert. Along with new herd animals, whose arrival in Africa preceded that of cultivated cereals by more than a thousand years, came new habits of mobility and heightened familiarity with the mineral-encrusted passes through the Egyptian and Nubian Deserts, where new materials awaited discovery. The story of the Neolithic in the Nile Valley is not, then, the expected one of migratory hunter-gatherers choosing to settle down in permanent villages, but rather one of settled fisher-hunter-foragers electing to go (conspicuously) on the move with their herds.

4

THE (FIRST) GLOBAL VILLAGE

The great transformations of humanity are only in part reported in terms of the revolutions in technology with resulting increases in the number of people living together.

Robert Redfield, *The Primitive World and its Transformations* (1953)

In his *Man Makes Himself* (1936), V. Gordon Childe, the most influential prehistorian of the twentieth century, identified two great revolutions in human history prior to the Industrial Revolution: the Neolithic Revolution, which saw the invention of farming, and the Urban Revolution of the fourth millennium BC, which saw amongst other things the invention of writing and the first experiments in large-scale cohabitation. In doing so he also—and inevitably, perhaps—created a fault-line in our understanding of prehistory, which has since obscured the momentous developments in village life that came after the origins of agriculture but preceded the Urban Revolution on the Mesopotamian plain. This much neglected phase in world history needs a name.

Perhaps it is best described as the first era of the 'global village', to literalize Marshall McLuhan's metaphor for the electronic age. It was a period in which regional distinctions collapsed in the face of new communication media, creating a kind of mass consciousness which was nevertheless contingent upon the localized enactment of concrete activities: specific ways of making and doing things within houses and villages.

In many ways, this fateful fifth millennium is a period of paradoxes. It has no clear parallels in the historical or ethnographic records of recent village societies. In the Mesopotamian lowlands it is known as the Ubaid period, after the site of Tell el-'Ubaid in southern Iraq. But its innovations were the outcome of interlocking developments across a much larger area, extending from the Cilician Gates, overlooking the Mediterranean, to the Gulf of Oman, on the Arabian Sea. It precedes the invention of the cuneiform script, and yet it crystallized the technological and social foundations upon which writing developed. It antedates the first cities, yet its settlements—sometimes smaller in scale than their Neolithic precursors, and rarely exceeding five hectares—already exhibit many features of urban life, such as specialized bureaucratic procedures and a complex division of craft activities. Its modes of consumption and exchange were also very different from those of earlier prehistory. They involved new media such as smelted and cast metals, wheel-finished pottery, and alcoholic drinks, bringing with them important changes—and no doubt disruptions—in social life. Implicit in all these developments was an acceleration in the rhythm of exchange between lowland villages and their highland and coastal neighbours.

The Beginnings of Metallurgy

Let us begin with metals, as their unique capacity for fusion and shape-shifting was central—both symbolically and practically—to the wider transformations in question. Copper, lead, gold, and silver were all known to early Neolithic societies in their native forms. They were initially valued (like exotic stones) as rare substances that could be cold-worked by hammering, rubbing, and incising. But the radical transformation of ores into metal by heat was achieved only in the fifth millennium BC. Gordon Childe described this discovery as the 'beginnings of chemistry', at the same time pointing out the aura of magic and ritual which must have surrounded the mutation of brittle stone into a tough, yet plastic medium.

As Mircea Eliade, the historian of religion, would later observe, this breakthrough had its roots in 'the demiurgic experiences of the primeval potter' (1978: 7). And it can be placed on a still longer continuum of technological discovery, which begins with the use of fire to transform raw flesh into cooked meat, a practice perhaps coeval with the evolution of culture itself. This long genealogy of human engagement with the effects of fire upon matter has had its impact on many areas of social life, including religion and language. Even today metalworkers talk of alloy 'recipes', just as Mesopotamian texts use words for cooking and roasting to describe the refinement of metal. This symbolic association of metalworking and cuisine can be traced back to the Ubaid period at Değirmentepe, in highland Turkey. There familiar household rituals provided a framework for the organization of metallurgical activities, with the forge becoming an extension of the domestic hearth.

In the case of metallurgy, unlike cooking food or firing clay, the resulting change of state (from solid, to glowing liquid, and back to solid) was *reversible*, and could be endlessly repeated with no loss of substance. It was this capacity for endless translation between distinct realms of meaning that differentiated metals from earlier commodities such as precious stones, whose forms could only be altered to new tastes by their progressive reduction through chipping or carving. Metalwork—even when cast into some locally meaningful shape—was never truly 'finished', but always carried residual significance as a commodity, capable of transferring its value to some new cultural context (consider the sad fate of Oscar Wilde's *Happy Prince*, whose statue body, stripped of its golden skin, is melted down for scrap).

The initial discovery of metallurgy could have been made in any number of places around the margins of the Fertile Crescent where fuel and metallic ores were obtainable in sufficient quantities. But only through its wide dissemination could metals become valued as a general medium of exchange. This accounts for the broadly simultaneous appearance, during the fifth millennium BC, of evidence for smelting, forging, casting, and alloying on the southern shores of the Caspian Sea (with access to the rich metal deposits of the Iranian Plateau), in the Turkish highlands above the Euphrates (close to the poly-metallic ores of the Taurus Mountains), and as far south as the arid margins of the Negev Desert (a few days journey from the copper sources of southern Jordan). The flow of metals around this circuit has been demonstrated through chemical analysis of a hoard of ornate copper artefacts—cast in the lost-wax technique—which was found in the Judean Desert of southern Israel. They contained traces of arsenic and antimony, the nearest sources of which lie 1000 kilometres distant, in eastern Turkey or Azerbaijan.

No less striking than the spread of metallurgical knowledge was the dissemination of new farming techniques. The practices of grafting and artificial pollinating, which form the basis of tree-crop horticulture, are widely in evidence by the end of the Ubaid period. Again it is difficult to identify a single point of origin for their development, and the techniques themselves may have long preceded their widespread application (there is tentative evidence, in Israel, for fig domestication at around 9000 BC). What distinguishes the fifth millennium is both the local intensification of these techniques and the cross-regional transfer of specific tree-crops around the Fertile Crescent: olive, fig, and almond spreading along the Syrian coast; vine and pomegranate across the foothills of the Taurus; and the date palm from the marshy head of the Persian Gulf. Such transfers reflect, not just the transmission of new farming methods, but also of new modes of consumption and social display, further reflected in a growing preference for wool textiles over earlier types of garment woven from flax. It is at this time that we detect the development of new sheep breeds with fleecy coats (as opposed to the naturally hairy varieties of the early Neolithic period), initially concentrated in the uplands of western Iran.

Villages into the Melting Pot

The combined result of all these changes, as Andrew Sherratt (1999) first pointed out, was a dramatic proliferation in the range of consumables available to prehistoric societies around the entire Fertile Crescent. Their creative hybridization generated entirely new food products—unprecedented flavours, smells, and sensations—and modes of personal appearance, just as the mixing of different metals created new materials with previously unknown properties of form and colour.

What was the role of the Mesopotamian lowlands in this process, which Sherratt has called 'the diversification of desire'? Lacking a distinct repertory of raw materials, villagers on the floodplains of the Tigris and Euphrates were nevertheless ideally positioned to play the role of go-between, mixing and matching commodities from regions as diverse as the mountains of Turkey and the coastal lagoons of the Persian Gulf. Particularly significant, as Sherratt noted, was the transfer of yeasts from cultivated fruits to malted cereals, which marked the beginnings of leavened bread and wheat beer (an innovation subsequently transferred—along with the grapevine—to another cereal-rich alluvial plain, that of Egypt, by the late fourth millennium BC). In adopting the role of inventive mediators, Mesopotamian villagers reshaped the social world of the household to increase productivity, disseminating new styles of consumption, and refining the techniques of commerce. Certain aspects of this process, which laid the cultural foundations of urban life, stand out with particular clarity in the archaeological record.

First of all, we are immediately struck by the homogenization of built environments in villages across the entire Mesopotamian plain. The resulting situation meant that a hypothetical villager from southern Iraq, entering a house 1000 kilometres away in the Turkish highlands, would have felt broadly at ease with the domestic arrangements he found there: a long, T-shaped hall with a focal hearth at one end, branching off into a series of side-chambers. He would also have recognized a familiar suite of ceramic serving utensils, such as handled drinking cups and spouted jars. Both vessel types were novelties of this period, and their spread implies the adoption of shared forms of hospitality, and perhaps also ritual practices, across a vast area. This new uniformity in pottery is partly accounted for by the adoption of the slow potter's wheel, a manually turned disc on a central pivot. Its use increased the output of decorated ceramics, and led to a degree of standardization in vessel shapes and ornamentation, accompanied by the disappearance of highly individualized handmade wares. Use of the wheel was also symptomatic of a new rigidity in the control of domestic crafts (and perhaps specifically of female labour), achieved through the spatial segregation of tasks within the household and the introduction of machinery that constrained movement.

The Changing Face of Clay

There is no evidence for the use of pack donkeys or ox-driven carts in the Near East until the fourth millennium BC, so the flow of goods between Ubaid villages may still have been relatively small scale. Trade was nevertheless subject to new forms of regulation through the use of special accounting devices and techniques of commodity marking, all of which were based upon a single medium of communication: the clay from which customary tokens of contract were formed, and which later bore the impression of seals and the earliest written signs.

Across the Fertile Crescent, clay figurines of pregnant women and domestic animals—together with geometric tokens—had, since Neolithic times, provided communities with a shared language of signification. Almost since the beginnings of farming the manual process of shaping, firing, and even breaking these miniature forms seems to have been closely linked to the conduct of important social transactions, perhaps involving exchanges of kin as well as animals and other goods. Around 7000 BC, in northern Mesopotamia, the symbolic role of clay in regulating commodity transfers was extended through the development of specialized sealing practices for storage vessels. This involved placing a band of wet clay over the mouth of a container and impressing it with a carved stone amulet (which did double service as a personal ornament), leaving a distinguishing mark that could be used to trace the product back to a particular individual or institution: a point of origin.

This seemingly innocuous development would have far-reaching consequences, still detectable in today's consumer cultures. The presence of a clay sealing demonstrated the integrity of the package and its contents, particularly important in the case of organic comestibles, and had the potential to reduce the risks involved in exchanges between unfamiliar partners. But it also introduced a new potential for mystification into the circulation and consumption of commodities. Then, as now, breaking a seal always disturbs a prior set of relationships: between the owner of the sealed object, the owner of the seal used to fasten it, and the agencies evoked by the image carved on the seal's surface, which were sometimes of a supernatural kind. It is therefore both something of a violation and something of a temptation, setting in motion a chain of consequences, the outcomes of which cannot always be foreseen, and may lead to misfortune. Seals have the potential to rewrite social history, and as such have often been viewed as portentous and dangerous objects in their own right.

Later Mesopotamian 'dream omens' credited them with magical powers, including the power to produce or destroy offspring.

As the range of commodities expanded during the Ubaid period, the miniature designs impressed onto their clay sealings became more vivid and diverse. Among them we find a new bestiary of real and fictitious animals in poses of violence or copulation, a panoply of scenes showing people drinking and feasting, and a hybrid figure with human body and ram's head, who holds aloft a pair of snakes. This rapidly expanding cast of characters—and the real human agents behind their production—now stood guard over the world of commodities, occupying an important space of the social imagination between products and their consumption. Once broken and removed from their containers, clay sealings could also be stored as records of transaction, and evidence from Tell Sabi Abyad in northern Syria suggests that this was an aspect of their use from the very beginning. New possibilities of control were thereby generated over a vital social commodity: the memory of relationships formed through the exchange of goods.

By the middle of the fourth millennium BC, another new commercial technique had been introduced, involving the enclosure of groups of miniature commodity tokens within hollow clay spheres known as *bullae*. The outer surfaces of these spheres bear the imprint of seals, and also of impressed numerical signs corresponding to the tokens within. The linked use of bullae, seals, and tokens was followed quite rapidly by the appearance of the first clay tablets impressed with numerical signs, and similarly overlain with seal impressions. Urban institutions, responsible for the organization of unprecedented numbers of people and things, provided a context within which the established role of clay as a recipient of signs was further abstracted from physical processes of storage and exchange. Here the stylus would soon come to supplement the seal, allowing abstract information to be classified, quantified, and otherwise manipulated in a bureaucratic manner.

The Dark Millennium

To summarize, the fifth millennium BC was a period of remarkable cultural symbiosis in the absence of marked urbanization or political centralization. The disruption of this pattern of development may have begun to the south of Mesopotamia, in the distinctive setting of the Persian Gulf, where current reconstructions suggest a significant—but localized—change in environmental conditions around this time. The Gulf is only 35 metres deep in most places, and much of it could be crossed on foot just 12,000 years ago. Since that time, its shallow basin—once no doubt densely inhabited by fishers, hunters, and foragers—had been gradually filling with waters from the Arabian Sea, pushing these groups into ever closer contact with the occupants of the Mesopotamian alluvium. Ubaid serving vessels and their local imitations are found as far south as the Straits of

Hormuz. Trading activity along these routes (in search of timber, metals, and precious stone) would surely have continued to expand eastwards towards the Indus, were it not for an episode of climatic deterioration which commenced around 4000 BC.

Archaeologists working in the Gulf refer to this episode as the 'dark millennium': a localized period of high aridity and site abandonment along the eastern Arabian coastline, which coincides suggestively with the Urban Revolution in Mesopotamia, and with the reorientation of Sumerian trade towards the north and east. Maritime links between Sumer and the Gulf of Oman, temporarily severed, would only be fully restored towards the onset of the Early Bronze Age (*c.*3000 BC). By that time, the aggressive northward expansion of Mesopotamian trading contacts along the Euphrates had decisively altered the fate of societies from Egypt to the deserts of central Asia.

5

ORIGIN OF CITIES

Go up, pace out the walls of Uruk,
Study the foundation terrace and examine the
  brickwork.
.   .   .   .

Three and a half square miles is the measure of
  Uruk!
[Search out] the foundation box of copper,
[Release] its lock of bronze,
Raise the lid upon its hidden contents...

> From the *Epic of Gilgamesh* (second
> millennium BC, translated by B. R. Foster)

A cuneiform text known as the Sumerian King List describes the descent of kingship from heaven into the cities of the Mesopotamian plain. Kingship comes down from on high as an unsolicited gift from the gods. Neither fully possessed nor reciprocated, its arrival on earth sets in motion a cycle of violence whereby one city in turn abducts it from another. Attested in various recensions from the late third into the second millennium BC, the King List precisely enumerates the time that each city

66

held onto kingship, from the millennia-long dominion of godlike heroes, such as Gilgamesh and the divine shepherd Dumuzi, to the reigns of mortal rulers whose years are counted on a human scale, and whose existence can often be corroborated from other sources. In constructing a mythical lineage for the dynastic powers of its day, the content of the King List is strongly conditioned by the political circumstances of its composition, and cannot be reliably used to reconstruct the political history of earlier periods. Nevertheless, its narrative structure, which takes the existence of cities as a given—requiring no explanation—reveals a pervasive attachment to urban life which finds only limited parallels in Egyptian literary sources, and has its roots in much earlier transformations.

The beginnings of urbanization in Mesopotamia can, in fact, be traced back a full two thousand years before the composition of the Sumerian King List, to the fourth millennium BC. Little is known about systems of government in these very earliest cities. The high ranking title of *en*—also documented from later periods—occurs in cuneiform texts from Uruk by the end of the fourth millennium, although its meaning may have changed considerably over the centuries. By the Early Dynastic period (*c.*3000–2350 BC), for which fuller records exist, it relates to the ruler's administrative and ritual duties in serving the cult of the city-god. At Ur the sovereign and military leader was termed *lugal* (literally: 'big man') and the term *ensi* carried a similar meaning in the city-state of Lagash. Archaeological evidence for the existence of palaces—in the sense of royal households distinct from the temples of the gods—has not been conclusively identified in Mesopotamia prior to the third millennium BC. In considering the nature of earlier forms of urban government we can look, with due circumspection, to other types of institution, which formed part of the fabric of city life in later periods. These included the major temples, with each city claiming a special—but not exclusive—relationship to a particular deity; the assemblies of city elders; wards located within the city walls but still organized on traditional family lines ('urban villages', as Nicholas Postgate (1992) calls them); and also mercantile organizations, based outside the fortifications in the city harbour. As I go on to discuss, however, it is the material record of the fourth millennium BC which—even in the absence of directly informative texts—provides our most reliable testimony to the nature of social and economic life in the world's first cities.

As a point of entry to the origin of cities in the fourth millennium BC, it is worth contemplating what becomes of a village-based society when individual households— the given units of social organization since Neolithic times—are increasingly unable to regulate the content of goods passing through them. The fifth millennium BC had been a period of spiralling experimentation and hybridization in dietary practices and material culture. It generated unprecedented diversity in the world of goods, but also introduced new uncertainties into the realm of domestic consumption and exchange. Many of the commodities now in wider circulation, notably dairy products and alcoholic drinks, were susceptible to natural deterioration as well as deliberate adulteration, and had potentially harmful effects when corrupted or wrongly consumed. The multiplication of products also generated new ambiguities concerning the origin of goods, which were amplified through the proliferation of commodity seals and labels—in a plethora of regional styles—among village communities. Metals too could be blended from multiple points of origin, and their circulation in cast and alloyed forms added a new liquidity (and unpredictability) to material transactions. Such transformations cannot be adequately circumscribed within the realm of 'economy'. They touch upon fundamental areas of social life such as trust, personal health, and hygiene. In this chapter I argue that the origin of cities, writing, and centralized institutions of unprecedented scale was in significant part a response to these uncertainties, pioneered on the southern alluvium of Mesopotamia.

Uruk, Handicraft of the Gods

Around four thousand years ago scribes in the Mesopotamian city of Nippur wrote down a myth about the origins of commerce. It is known as *Enmerkar and the Lord of Aratta*. Enmerkar is introduced as the king and builder of the Sumerian city of Unug. This is the city called Uruk in the Akkadian language, and also in modern archaeological parlance. In the Hebrew Book of Genesis it appears under the name of Erech—alongside

Babel, Akkad, and Calneh—as one of the primeval kingdoms of Shinar (Sumer), the land settled after the Great Flood, and the setting for the ill-fated episode at the Tower of Babel. In the Sumerian epic, the Lord of Aratta lives in a distant highland region where the environmental conditions of Sumer are reversed. Grain is scarce, but the mountains yield an endless harvest of precious metals and stones. In the absence of trade and writing, whose origins are linked in the story, Enmerkar must obtain these goods to furnish a dwelling for the goddess Inanna, and secure her favour. This he achieves by answering a series of challenges. He must send a cargo of grain to Aratta in open, porous nets; fashion a sceptre from a material that is not wood, reed, metal, or any known stone; and match the fighting dog of the Lord of Aratta with a dog of his own, whose coat is of an unknown colour and pattern. Enmerkar finds ingenious technical solutions to all these problems. He fills the nets with sprouted barley, fabricates a new material for the sceptre, and (a little fraudulently) manufactures an elaborate textile to act as a new coat (in both senses!) for the dog. Salvation for the city comes through the inventive use and transformation of local resources, and the plot concludes with Inanna's decision to institute peaceful trade between Uruk and Aratta.

Like all myths, *Enmerkar and the Lord of Aratta* deftly combines elements of the real and the unreal. Attempting to unravel fact from fantasy is unwise. It may then be no more than serendipity that the site of Uruk—identified over a century ago with the mound of Warka in southern

Iraq—has come to occupy a central place in modern understandings of the emergence of cities and writing. Excavations there have produced evidence for the earliest development of the cuneiform script (*c*.3300–3000 BC) in the form of tablets documenting the management of commodities and labour by large urban institutions, which were concentrated within a walled precinct atop the centre of the mound. Archaeological survey of the surrounding landscape suggests that by this time the city had already grown to around 250 hectares, dwarfing other settlements on the Mesopotamian plain, and perhaps containing as many as 20,000 residents. Some archaeologists now prefer the term 'Uruk Expansion' over Gordon Childe's 'Urban Revolution' as a label for this process. The reason is that the urbanization of Uruk is associated with an equally striking spread of southern Mesopotamian cultural influence over much of the Fertile Crescent.

On first impression, the effect seems akin to that of a volcanic eruption. By the late fourth millennium BC the lowland plains of south-west Iran appear totally submerged, their major centres (such as Susa) engulfed by Sumerian products. Along the Syrian Euphrates appear new settlements, such as the 10-hectare site of Habuba Kabira, a miniature Uruk in every respect, other than the absence of cuneiform writing. On the adjacent, rain-fed plains of northern Mesopotamia, southern manufactures began to replace or supplement local products. Still wider impacts can be traced as a series of ever-thinning ripples, washing over the Taurus and Zagros

Mountains towards the Black Sea and the Iranian Plateau, and spilling into the Mediterranean where small quantities of Mesopotamian goods were projected as far south as Upper Egypt. The latter included commodity seals, which were quickly adapted for use with local vessel forms.

On closer inspection, however, this spread begins to look less like an indiscriminate eruption, and more like an escalating series of strategic advances from south to north. Many of the areas affected had themselves been moving steadily towards urban life for some centuries, and possessed local systems of bureaucratic management which—although still non-literate—were a direct outgrowth of Ubaid practices such as the use of seals and standardized metrical systems. The expansion of Uruk 'colonies' and 'outposts', as Guillermo Algaze (1993) terms them, follows a commercial logic. They occupied the interstices of important trade corridors, both overland and riverine. Where no such gaps existed, they intruded directly into the heart of existing local settlements, large and small, from the Upper Euphrates to the highlands of western Iran. Archaeologists recognize these intrusions by the appearance of Uruk-style buildings, storage and serving vessels, and accounting devices among otherwise local forms of material culture. This was by no means the first great colonial venture in human history, among which we must count the initial expansion of our species throughout the globe, and the subsequent displacement of hunter-gatherer groups by Neolithic farmers. It was, however, the first instance of a type of colonial movement—familiar from more recent eras—in which entire communities budded off from an urban metropolis, re-establishing themselves in distant locations, yet maintaining distinct identities and regular trade relations that linked them to their cities of origin.

A similar ability to maintain extended communities over great areas lay at the heart of the Harappan cultural expansion, within and beyond the Indus Valley, a thousand years later (c.2600–1800 BC). The two networks—Uruk and Harappan—share other similarities which hint at common, underlying principles of organization. In both cases evidence for hereditary inequalities between different sectors of the population (e.g. in the form of rich dynastic burials) is conspicuous by its absence. And in both cases there is a remarkable similarity of form between settlements of all sizes within the commercial network. Very large sites such as Mohenjo-daro, in the Sind province of Pakistan, and Uruk (both about 250 hectares) are essentially scaled up versions of very small or even tiny ones, a few hectares or less in size. As Daniel Miller (1985) observed some time ago, to find any kind of similarity in the layout of sites so widely differing in scale suggests something significant about the societies in question.

No less striking is what Miller refers to as a 'lack of individualization' in the realm of material culture, from house forms (including the use of uniform dimensions for mud-bricks) to ceramic vessels, across sites of all scales. Hence the massive building complexes that occupy the central walled district of Uruk (known as 'Eanna' in later periods) follow the long-established tripartite plan of ordinary households, lending credence to the view that they were conceived as 'Houses of the Gods' on an immemorial model of village life. Ritual practices generated through the routines of domestic activity—and concerned with such everyday household matters as personal hygiene, storage, hospitality, and food preparation—appear in each case to have been reproduced on a monumental scale, and with an emphasis on collective rather than exclusive participation. Consider, for example, the great assembly halls of the Eanna complex at Uruk, accommodating up to three hundred people at a time, or the vast bathing facilities at the heart of Mohenjo-daro. (In an earlier study I have tried to show how a similar story—with hierarchical institutions emerging out of the micro-practices of daily life—can be told for Egypt, but with a special emphasis upon the body itself as metaphor and mediator of relationships between kings, gods, and mortals; see Wengrow 2006, and also Chapter 8.)

The process of magnification, however, also involved significant changes in the character of collective life, which are particularly visible in the relations between the living and the dead. Human remains are near absent from sites within the Uruk cultural network, and are similarly rare within the Harappan cultural zone. The dead, it seems, were expelled from the space of the living and removed to special burial grounds outside the walls of the settlement, perhaps exemplified by the funerary site of Tell Majnuna near the city of Nagar (Tell Brak) in northern Syria. Comparable reforms in the treatment of the dead are known to have accompanied urbanization in other, better-documented periods of history. Philippe Ariès (1994) reports, for example, that Roman law codes 'forbade burial *in urbe*, within the city... so that the *sanctitas* of the inhabitants' homes would be preserved'; and the Early Church Fathers would later argue that intramural burial polluted 'the very limbs of Christ' (that is, the City of God and its inhabitants, created in His image). The increasingly systematic expulsion of the dead from Mesopotamian settlements during the fourth millennium BC indicates that the growth of cities was associated with new concepts of purity and contagion, which also had implications for the world of commodities.

The Wheels of Commerce

The emergence of cities in Mesopotamia coincides with a range of innovations in large-scale commerce and extensive farming. Their distribution extended far beyond Mesopotamia itself, and formed part of a wider technological milieu from which emerged the distinctive forms of both Egyptian and Sumerian society. The use of pack donkeys is attested in surrounding regions, from Egypt to highland Iran, by *c.*3300 BC. Around the same time evidence for the adoption of cattle-drawn ploughs appears across a truly enormous area, from farming communities dispersed along the Neolithic fringes of

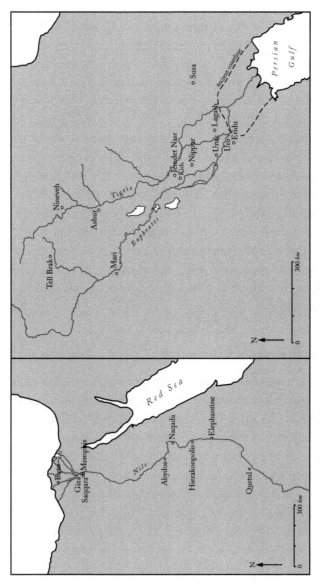

Map 5. Major sites in Egypt and Mesopotamia, c.4000 to 2000 BC

northern Europe to the cities of the Sumerian plain. Wheeled carts, also drawn by cattle, are depicted on some of the earliest written documents from Uruk, and a new interest in the industrial application of rotary power is further reflected in the use of the potter's flywheel (driven by hand) to produce standardized packaging, suitable for the bulk transport of liquid commodities. (The bow-drill was a much earlier, Neolithic invention, while the lapidary engraving wheel was a later innovation of the second millennium bc, as was the use of a foot-powered wheel for throwing pots.) Intensification of ceramic production is also evident in the adoption of modular, factory-line processes of assembly for standard vessel forms, particularly liquid containers. Along with these developments we find an important refinement in the marking of sealed commodities, which served to further distinguish Uruk products from those of neighbouring regions. In place of stamp seals, use of which continued elsewhere, Uruk and its colonial offshoots employed cylindrical seals engraved with intaglio designs. The more complex of these designs were technological marvels in their own right: masterpieces of lapidary carving, all the more astonishing (and difficult to counterfeit) for the fact that they were rendered in reverse, so as to produce a correct impression when rolled over the clay sealing of a commodity vessel.

In pursuing new commercial strategies, cities on the southern alluvium enjoyed a unique combination of advantages. Under irrigation the extraordinary fertility of river-borne soils provided surplus cereal crops to feed a centralized workforce, and for conversion into more sophisticated comestibles (varieties of bread and beer). The wetlands around the head of the Persian Gulf—teeming with fish, crabs, and turtles—added an important source of protein to the urban diet, while consumption of meat and dairy products was reserved for festive occasions. Major centres such as Uruk, Larsa, Ur, and Eridu also sat astride the confluence of three major axes of water transport: the Euphrates and Tigris Rivers, and a network of east–west contacts crossing the marshy profile of the Gulf, then located some 200 kilometres inland of its present location. To place these early cities in their proper environmental context today requires an effort of the imagination. The lateral movement of the Tigris and Euphrates beds over the past few thousand years has left their ruins high and dry above the central desert of southern Iraq. But their walled defences were once arrayed along the fringes of a maritime seaboard, and the deep scars of river canals which coursed through the heart of their sacred precincts are still clearly visible at sites such as Nippur—the seat of the Enlil, overlord of the Sumerian pantheon—sitting watch over the northern frontier of the alluvium.

In his (1993) *The Uruk World System*, Guillermo Algaze offers an explanation for the Uruk Expansion of the fourth millennium BC that would no doubt have found approval with the author(s) of *Enmerkar and the Lord of Aratta*. The key, he argues, lay in the competitive export of labour-intensive goods manufactured from locally abundant resources: principally dyed and woven textiles, and processed consumables such as alcoholic drinks, dairy products, unguents, animal fats, and oils, which feature widely in the earliest cuneiform records from Uruk. Wool textiles—durable and lightweight products, easily transported, and able to absorb the value added by skilled weavers, fullers, and dyers—were particularly crucial in this regard, as they would prove to be millennia later in laying the foundations of the Industrial Revolution in Europe. Detailed documentation of the textile industry and its central role in long-distance trade is available from the third millennium BC, by which time the palace and temple estates of Sumer were routinely processing raw wool by the thousands of tons, using an encumbered (largely female) workforce.

A proportion of finished textiles was regularly traded onwards by networks of specialized merchants, reaching centres of consumption as far as central Anatolia (modern Turkey) where the business archives of a later Assyrian trading colony (c.1900 BC) have survived at the site of Kanesh, near modern Kayseri. They reveal a scrupulously organized bilateral trade—supported by complex credit arrangements between multiple urban stakeholders—with tin (an essential component of bronze) and fine textiles moving northwards onto the Anatolian plateau by donkey caravan, and a regular flow of gold and silver moving back in the other direction to the city of Ashur, on the northern reaches of the Tigris. Silver, from the mid-third millennium onwards, was highly valued as a standard measure of exchange in lowland Mesopotamia, used in transfers of fixed and mobile property. Assyrian (north Mesopotamian) traders were thus able to generate substantial profits by using relatively small amounts of Anatolian silver to purchase bulk quantities of tin and textiles from production centres further south. These commodities were then traded back over the Taurus mountains into central Turkey, where they were in high demand, in return for large shipments of silver (acquired at a highly favourable rate of exchange), which could be reinvested in the purchase of new merchandise to support further commercial ventures of the same kind. This was Bronze Age venture capitalism at its finest.

Algaze suggests that, by the late fourth millennium BC, the consumers of Mesopotamian export goods already formed an extended supply chain, filtering raw materials (such as metals, timber, and precious stones) from a vast catchment area towards the urban centres of the southern alluvium. We thus find Uruk enclaves of varying scale occupying highland passes through the Zagros (the corridors to the copper resources of the Iranian Plateau, and beyond them the lapis mines of Afghanistan), and the Taurus Mountains above the Upper Euphrates (en route to Anatolian deposits of copper, silver, and gold). The argument is convincing in its essentials, but leaves open a fundamental question: why would products manufactured in southern Mesopotamia have been especially desirable in the first place? After all, many of the goods concerned were already locally produced in neighbouring regions, and were therefore being exported on what amounts to a 'coals to

Newcastle' basis. To address this question, we should examine more closely the contents of the earliest written documents from Uruk. First, though, it is necessary to briefly define what is and is not meant by 'writing' in this context.

Writing: The 'Spiritualism of the State'

In the story of Enmerkar, composed a thousand years after the invention of the cuneiform script, writing is invented to convey a challenge from the King of Uruk to the Lord of Aratta. The king's speech is too long for his messenger to remember, so Enmerkar—ever the innovator—inscribes it on a tablet of clay. Given our modern reliance on writing to convey language at a distance, we might find this a plausible context for the origins of writing itself; but we would be wrong.

The earliest cuneiform inscriptions are in fact made up largely of ideograms; graphic symbols that represent ideas rather than units of language such as phonemes. They are usually combined with numerical and metro-logical symbols, and among them we find signs for a wide range of domestic animals, birds, fish, plants, stones, types of metal (and metal artefacts), textiles, dairy products, and professional roles and titles. But the structural arrangement of these signs does not follow the linear structure of natural speech, and was never intended to do so. Instead it uses a visual format attuned to mathematical notation, dividing the surface of the tablet into boxes arranged in vertical columns, each containing a combination of ideograms and numerals. This is readily explained by the bureaucratic, book-keeping functions that cuneiform writing was originally designed to fulfil. The 'muse' which inspired its inventors was not epic poetry, song, or royal decrees, but the no less compelling language of commodity flows, into and out of the great households of the earliest cities. The subsequent adaptation of cuneiform writing to represent the grammar and syntax of spoken language, and eventually to record literature, took centuries to unfold. A major stimulus came around the middle of the third millennium BC, when the script was increasingly used to write elements of non-Sumerian languages, such as the Semitic languages used at Ebla and Mari in Syria: cultural mixing and blending, once again, the mother of invention.

Karl Marx described bureaucracy as 'the spiritualism of the state', creating a carefully patrolled domain of phantom entities—signs that stand for beings and things—to exist alongside real people and objects. The earliest written signs were of precisely this nature, standing in for concrete things rather than units of speech, and signifying their changing relationships within a closed system where number, order, and rank were the only significant dimensions of value. In Egypt, as I have discussed more fully elsewhere (Wengrow 2006), the emergence of writing had a similarly close relationship with the world of commodities. As in Mesopotamia, script invention was tied to the standardization of material goods, and to the adoption of specialized marking systems—including the use of cylinder seals, an imported technique—to classify and differentiate types of produce. Most of the earliest known hieroglyphic inscriptions relate in one way or another to the differentiation and ranking of consumables. They appear on labels, seals, or other marks which—applied to the surface of ordinary, mass-produced commodity containers—served to ascribe special origins of one sort or another to their contents, identifying them as products of royal estates, as exotic luxuries, or as 'the best' of a given type of produce. In Egypt, the early development of these marking systems was directly associated with the organization and performance of elite funerary rituals, in which vast quantities of wealth were taken out of circulation to furnish the tombs of deceased kings and courtiers: a striking case of bureaucracy in the service of sacrifice.

In order for such parallel worlds of administrative representation to function, real objects and sentient beings (both human and animal) also had to undergo a degree of change in the direction of uniformity: one vessel, unit of metal, or head of cattle the same as another. The great number of non-numerical signs in the early cuneiform corpus from Uruk indicates strong cultural resistance to the imposition of such a rigid scheme of order. More than 1,500 ideograms are attested, and many are only infrequently used. But the turn towards standardization nevertheless had far-reaching effects upon Mesopotamian economy and society.

Sacred Commodities: The Mesopotamian Origins of Product Branding

In total, some five thousand cuneiform documents, dating between 3300 and 3000 BC, have been recovered from the site of Uruk. Other centres on the southern alluvium have yielded much smaller numbers. A small proportion are lists of terms for particular types of wood, metal, dairy products, etc., as well as terms for professional crafts and statuses within the urban administration. These inventories most probably served as mnemonic aids, and provide an insight into the nature of scribal training. Most of the surviving documents, however, are either short receipts for goods or more consolidated accounts, which were originally compiled into business archives. After the information they contained ceased to have any useful function, these archives were dumped in the vicinity of the Eanna complex, or used as ballast in the construction of later buildings.

From their contents it can nevertheless be deduced that a primary application of the writing system lay in distinguishing between subclasses of products on the basis of their constituent materials, ingredients, and labour. Labour was itself quantified in standard, commoditized units of timekeeping, from which our own sixty-minute hour is ultimately derived. And the same system of calculation was extended to particular goods, notably grain, with time values such as months and days doing double service as standard commodity units. Among the goods in question we find cheese, butter oil, and fat enumerated in various grades and flavoured varieties. Some eighty varieties of fish, used as sources of oil and dried protein, are recorded. But by far the most common accounts deal with disbursements of grain, including semi-processed forms such as barley malt, groats, and flour, used to produce fermented cereal products (types of bread and beer). Fine-grained classifications of finished goods reflect distinctions of purity, strength, and taste, further enhanced by the addition of condiments and spices. The scribes also distinguished woven products by fineness of mesh and weight, and certain high quality types of wool and finished textile were designated 'fit for the *en*': an important administrative role which, as previously noted, probably also included the presentation of offerings to the cult statue of the city god.

What more, then, can be inferred about the institutions responsible for producing these accounts? Clearly they were in a position to influence the flow of labour and resources between various sectors of the Sumerian economy, even if most aspects of productive life were physically located elsewhere, in other parts of the city or beyond its walls. Exact measurements and classifications of ingredients in the texts further indicate that products passing through these urban institutions were subject to systems of quality control, differentiating them from less closely regulated varieties of the same goods, which were widely available elsewhere. The cuneiform signs for food products are often depictions of the ceramic containers in which they were stored and transported, suggesting that packaging had itself become a strong marker of identity for finished products. And containers, in turn, were sealed with mechanically produced images linking them to prominent public institutions. Many of these images, applied with cylinder seals, appear to address concerns of provenance and trust quite directly. Some depict people at work in the manufacture of ceramics, dairy products, and textiles (closely associated with female labourers, shown with distinctive pig-tail hairstyles). Others depict a standardized male figure with a beard, turban and woven skirt—perhaps to be identified with the *en* of contemporary written docu-ments—engaged in collecting and transporting finished goods, or dedicating them to a temple: an act which implied their suitability for inclusion within the regular regime of offerings made to the gods.

Seals were to surface imagery what the reusable casting mould was to the production of three-dimensional objects: works of art in the first age of mechanical repro-duction, as Walter Benjamin might have put it, had he looked beyond the Classical Greeks. Analyses of the clay sealings from Uruk-period containers show that they sometimes travelled hundreds of kilometres with the products to which they were attached, but their application would have been no less significant for local urban consumers. Theirs was already a world of stand-ardized goods, quite familiar to us in some respects. Most of the finished products that surrounded them in everyday life no longer carried any visible trace of their producers' individual identities, owing to the division of production processes along extended chains of specialized labour. And the complex blending of ingredients and raw materials from multiple sources further ensured that the origin of goods had become increasingly hard to discern.

In much the same way as modern brand labels, seal images addressed these new uncertainties by creating fictional biographies—often of sacred origin—for goods which were otherwise anonymous. No doubt seals were also used for other, more straightforwardly bureaucratic purposes, such as the authorization of economic accounts. But they nevertheless formed part of what we are fully justified in referring to as the world's first 'brand economy', addressing a paradox which has since remained common to all large-scale economic systems, both capitalist and non-capitalist, from the origin of cities to the present: the paradox of living in a society made up of individual actors, whose relationships must nevertheless be formed and sustained through the circulation of impersonal goods.

6

FROM THE GANGES TO THE DANUBE: THE BRONZE AGE

> Thus, studies of world-systems must consider how the economic can be encompassed by the cultural and the sacred.
>
> Philippe Beaujard, 'The Indian Ocean in Eurasian and African World-Systems before the Sixteenth Century' (2005)

Geologists have a technical term for the vast band of highland mineral resources which extends, continuously, from the Alps to the Himalayas, before it descends towards the Indian Ocean. Steering its way through the Caucasus and Zagros ranges, and then sweeping up to the Pamirs (the 'Roof of the World') the 'Eurasian metallogenic belt' comprises—at various points along its length—deposits of gold, silver, copper, and tin (a necessary component, with copper, in the manufacture of bronze). Thrown up by the clash of the Eurasian and Afro-Arabian tectonic plates in the Mesozoic era, it straddles the area occupied 200 million years ago by a long-extinct body of water known as the Tethyan Ocean. On its east–west journey, the metallogenic belt traverses widely differing ecologies. As a result, the mineral riches of one quarter of the world are scattered from temperate valleys to subtropical coastlines, as though by some trickster at the dawn of time. But, as I go on to describe, what the primeval movements of the Earth's crust had pulled apart, the humanly constructed world of the Bronze Age—a world increasingly dominated by predatory elites—conspired to reunite.

The Transformation of Western Eurasia, *c.*3000–2000 BC

For archaeologists, the 'Bronze Age' has become a conventional term of reference for the third and second millennia BC in the Near East. The roots of the term, however, lie in the classification of European prehistory, where time must be measured without the aid of written sources. In origin it forms part of the chronological scheme known as the 'Three Age System'—Stone, Bronze, Iron—first devised in the early nineteenth century to reflect the changing sequence of cutting implements in the archaeological record. A side effect of this scheme in Europe was to tie the study of chronology to the study of technological change, conceived as a progressive narrowing of the limits to human intervention in the natural world. Specialists in the study of ancient Egypt and Mesopotamia, working mainly with texts and visual representations, use a different style of chronology based upon the reconstructed sequences of dynastic reigns. Here royal proclamations and King Lists tend to drown out the clamour of pots, tools, and weapons. Hence what archaeologists call the 'Early Bronze Age'—broadly the third millennium BC— encompasses the 'Early Dynastic' phase in Mesopotamia and the 'Old Kingdom' of Egypt, as well as the periods either side of them, which have their own conventional names and subdivisions (see Chronology Chart).

The great river valleys of the Nile, Tigris–Euphrates, and Indus have traditionally been viewed as isolated cradles of Bronze Age civilization, separated by vast tracts of thinly populated land. Surrounding regions— such as the Persian Gulf and the great intermontane basins of Central Asia—were long regarded as dormant spaces, patiently awaiting the dawn of the Silk and Spice Routes in the first millennium BC. Urban life was assumed to have sprung up only in regions of exceptional agricultural potential, where a dominant river course compressed people and local resources into symbiotic relationships. Over the past few decades, as a result of new fieldwork, it has become apparent that this picture must be jettisoned. Egypt, Mesopotamia, and the Indus were indeed major centres of population and innovation in the Early Bronze Age, but they were not alone.

By 2500 BC a network of walled cities such as Shahdad and Shahr-i Sokhta—comparable in magnitude to those of the Mesopotamian lowlands—extended across the

Iranian Plateau, occupying large internal drainage basins on the margins of forbidding deserts (the Dasht-e Kavir and the Dasht-e Lut). Towns such as Tepe Yahya and Tal-i Malyan had also sprung up on the overland routes between Mesopotamia and the Makran coast, sandwiched within rain-fed fluvial valleys between the dense folds of the Zagros Mountains. Far to the north existed other alluvial enclaves formed by run-off from the wall of mountains (the Elburz and Kopet Dagh) that bridges the Anatolian Plateau and the Hindu Kush: inland deltas—among them the Zeravshan, Tedzen, and Murghab of Turkmenistan—flowing into the dark sands of the Kyzylkum and Karakum Deserts. Urban settlement on their fertile soils shifted gradually from west to east during the course of the third millennium, culminating in the fortified 'oasis cities' of Bactria and Margiana (c.2100–1800 BC). These great walled enclosures, with their eye-catching bastions and burgeoning craft workshops, maintained contacts with the pastoral nomads of the Eurasian steppe, whose seasonal migrations extended to the frontiers of China. At much the same time (c.2200 BC) towns of considerable size and sophistication emerged in the Persian Gulf, from the northern coastal strip of Oman to the island of Bahrain (historical *Dilmun*).

The common features of these new urban worlds are more easily defined than the differences between them—differences of social and ritual organization, which reflect their diverse ecologies and cultural foundations. Each commanded access to a broad spectrum of resources, including agricultural products to sustain local manufacturing industries as well as key commodities such as metals and precious stones obtained from nearby highlands. All occupied niches of fertile farmland, fed by a variety of artesian and river-borne waters, and strategically located upon major trade routes extending between the great alluvial plains of the Punjab and Mesopotamia. And all shared certain basic techniques of commerce, whose lineage can be traced back to the Uruk Expansion: the use of seals (each major urban network had its own distinct repertory of commodity marks), mass production of wheel-made ceramics in standard volumes, and the circulation of metal ingots as currency. Systems of metrology, which have been carefully reconstructed from the stone weights found on archaeological sites, were also common to all. Given this striking range of similarities, it seems likely that other techniques of economic organization such as the management of farming estates were widely shared. Detailed information is lacking, however, outside Mesopotamia. A further network of fortified settlements, smaller in scale but similar in organization, stretched across the great landmass of Anatolia, bridging the waters of the northern Aegean and extending towards the frontiers of temperate Europe. The kingdom of Egypt, too, was part of this extended family of societies, but as I go on to discuss in Chapter 8 it also differed in important ways from its urban neighbours in Eurasia.

Relationships between these various regions go beyond formal resemblances. Each formed one segment in an extensive—albeit loosely integrated—commercial network, comprising both land and sea routes, which linked the economic fate of societies from the eastern Mediterranean to the foothills of the Himalayas. A wide range of commodities, notably metals, circulated continuously among them, and tools of commerce such as seals and weights moved freely between them, as did the major techniques of bulk transport (pack-donkey caravans, ox-driven carts, and sailing ships), all of which crystallized between the fourth and third millennia BC. Cities in the Indus Valley shared the same metrological standard as trading entrepots in the Persian Gulf, whose scales of measurement were in turn compatible with those of lowland Mesopotamia as far north as Ebla, and perhaps even beyond. This was trade on a scale of magnitude, and at a level of sophistication, which is still too often regarded as a unique feature of the modern world.

Links in a Chain: The Role of Bronze

As a designation of technological change, the Bronze Age must be handled with care. Bronze—an artificial alloy of copper and tin—is superior to pure copper in its mechanical properties. The addition of tin increases hardness, making sturdier weapons and sharper cutting implements, and also lowers the overall melting point, making casting easier. It was once widely supposed that the discovery of these technical advantages led to a rapid diffusion of bronze technology from the Near East to central Europe, where bronzes (made from tin extracted in the German Erzgebirge) begin to appear around 2300 BC. But it is now apparent that the mechanical properties of pure copper were superseded long before the discovery of tin-bronze at the beginning of the third millennium BC. The first enhancements, beginning more than a thousand years earlier, were achieved by smelting arsenic-rich copper ores, which produce a material comparable to bronze in hardness and ease of casting. On the Iranian Plateau, with its rich ore deposits, arsenic copper remained the preferred medium for cutting implements well into the Bronze Age. Egypt also resisted the new alloy until the second millennium BC and appears to have accorded it a value lower than pure (unalloyed) copper, which was favoured for the manufacture of royal and divine statuary, and other equipment used in ritual dedications.

Even in those areas where tin-bronze was adopted, mechanical efficiency seems to have played little role in its initial uptake. During the third millennium BC the new material was most enthusiastically embraced in three specific locations: the Mesopotamian lowlands, central Anatolia, and the northern Aegean (including the coastal promontory around Troy, and neighbouring islands). In all three regions its appearance coincides with an increased consumption of gold, and with the arrival of a brace of new techniques for the production of highly ornamental metalwork. Vessels and elaborate items of personal display—including a dazzling variety of pins, rings, diadems, head-dresses, necklaces, and bracelets—dominate these assemblages. Among them we find some of the earliest examples of decorative techniques for jewellery still widely in use today such as granulation, stone-setting, gilding, and chasing, many of them pioneered in the urban workshops of Mesopotamia. In its mode of consumption, bronze was then initially closer to gold and lapis lazuli (Chapter 2) than to utilitarian copper, from which it was visually distinguished by its lighter hue. And this is further reflected in its contexts of deposition. The trail of bronze-finds between Sumer and the Aegean is a series of jumps between richly laden tombs and concealed treasures, from the Royal Tombs of Ur to the hoards of Troy, and the carefully hidden jewellery deposits of Poliochni and Aigina. This last collection of objects, buried beneath a house floor at the site of Kolonna, contained a distinctive type of carnelian bead with etched decoration, originating in the workshops of the Indus Valley.

Historians of metallurgy Tamara Stech and Vincent Pigott (1986) have argued that the selection of bronze as an elevated medium of display was closely linked to the restricted manner of its acquisition, and the political control thereby exercised over its circulation. Together with gold and lapis lazuli, much of the tin used in the Near East during the Early Bronze Age was extracted from alluvial deposits in the distant highlands of Afghanistan, though sources also existed in the Zagros Mountains of western Iran. The movement of all three materials can be linked to the revival of Sumerian maritime trade in the Persian Gulf and its eastward extension at the end of the fourth millennium BC. Merchants based in the Indus Valley seem likely to have acted as mediators in this trade, maintaining a strategic presence at the confluence of the Amu Darya (Oxus) and Kokcha Rivers in northern Afghanistan, where a remote outpost of Harappan culture has been discovered at the site of Shortugai. But the question remains: why, at the beginning of the third millennium, was an artificially produced material added to the existing suite of luxury metals already in circulation? Stech and Pigott suspect an economic motive, linked to the increasing importance of another metal—silver—in the Mesopotamian economy.

By around 2500 BC, as I noted in Chapter 5, silver had achieved the status of currency among the urban elites of the Mesopotamian lowlands. The palace archives from Ebla document its circulation in standard units (cast ingots classified and no doubt hallmarked according to purity) totalling amounts that sometimes exceeded several tons in a single transfer. Silver was recognized as a medium for the purchase of both landed and moveable property, and its price was linked to that of gold. But whereas tin sources were concentrated far to the east of Sumer, supplies of silver lay to the west in precisely those areas which followed Mesopotamian fashions by adopting tin-bronze for prestige display: central Anatolia, and the northern Aegean. The commercial significance of bronze, then, begins to come into clearer focus. Unlike copper or gold, which were locally available in Anatolia, this was a manufactured substance over which Mesopotamian elites exercised a tight trade monopoly. So long as that monopoly was maintained, bronze could be used as a visual marker of their exclusive status for both domestic audiences and foreign trade partners. For the small but competitive communities of Anatolia and the Aegean, silver was a convenient price to pay for membership of this illustrious club, whose entry card was the display of bronze upon the bodies of the living and the dead and also, no doubt, on those of gods and heroes.

Sumerian Storehouses of the Gods

Only a tiny proportion of the metallic wealth that circulated between urban centres of the Early Bronze Age has been preserved in the archaeological record. Insights into the appearance of finished metalwork can be gained only from exceptional contexts, such as royal burials. (With the emergence of palaces and dynastic elites, the elite dead—long banished from urban spaces—resumed their old places of power within Mesopotamian households.) Currency forms of metal, such as standard ingots, have hardly survived at all. The reason for this is that, relative to the vast quantities attested in contemporary written sources, very little metal wealth was permanently withdrawn from circulation by urban elites.

There were of course great centres of accumulation, notably temples and palaces, where large quantities of metal were held in temporary storage. As with modern banking, the accumulation of capital involved—not just bureaucracy—but also a strong element of faith and trust, reinforced by ritual. The stability of temples as foci of trade and investment was grounded in the working fiction that their true assets would never be fully realized and were (theoretically) without limit. Each Mesopotamian temple was a storehouse of the gods, 'eternally possessing silver and lapis lazuli', as a Sumerian hymn to the Temple of Bau at Lagash puts it. This fiction was sustained through their additional role as Houses of the Gods, whose statues were located there and received regular gifts of food, clothing, and valuables. Such observances were intended to ensure the god's presence within the temple, and to demonstrate its institutional well being. The stockpiling of assets was thereby represented as an extension of the moral obligation to feed the gods (Chapter 7), whose sacred dwellings dominated the landscape of lowland urban centres and were poetically likened to mountains, the natural—and seemingly inexhaustible—sources of metals and minerals (among the ceremonial names given to Mesopotamian temples we find 'House, Skilfully Built Mountain' and 'House, Pure Mountain'). But accumulation was always temporary. Stored metallic wealth, when not mobilized as currency for trading ventures, was an important source of patronage and symbolic capital, especially when reintroduced to society in the form of prestigious display items such as weapons and jewellery, crafted by temple or palace artisans.

The looting of temples was an increasingly common feature of intercity rivalry in Early Dynastic Mesopotamia, and forms a recurring trope in the Sumerian literary genre of lamentation texts:

The leader of Umma...sacked the Bagara temple and looted its precious metals and lapis lazuli; he set fire to the Dugru temple and looted its precious metals and lapis lazuli; he sacked the Abzu'eg; he set fire to the temple of Gatumdug, looted its precious metals and lapis lazuli, and destroyed its statuary; he set fire to the shrine Eanna of Inanna, looted its precious metals and lapis lazuli and destroyed its statuary.

(Excerpt from the lament for the temples of Lagash; after Cooper 1986)

In another lament the goddess Ningal is made to weep over what remains of her devastated house in the city of Ur, and again the loss of silver and precious stone is identified as a particular source of trauma:

My possessions, like a flock of rooks rising up, have risen in flight—I shall cry 'O my possessions'. He who came from the south has carried my possessions off to the south—I shall cry 'O my possessions'. He who came from the highlands has carried my possessions off to the highlands—I shall cry 'O my possessions'. My silver, gems and lapis lazuli have been scattered about—I shall cry 'O my possessions'. The swamp has swallowed my treasures—I shall cry 'O my possessions'. Men ignorant of silver have filled their hands with my silver. Men ignorant of gems have fastened my gems around their necks.

(Excerpt from the lament for Ur; after Black et al. 2006)

Here the agents of destruction do not come from a rival city-state, but from the swamps and highlands beyond the alluvium, where the true value of silver and exotic stone is said to be unknown. In portraying these distant societies as ignorant barbarians and despoilers of wealth, the literary lament over Ur undoubtedly reflects the cultural perspective of an aggrieved, city-dwelling elite. But other forms of evidence, archaeological rather than textual, suggest that the disparities between urban and non-urban notions of value were more subtle and varied in character, particularly as regards the consumption of metallic wealth.

On the Margins of the System: Revisiting the 'Barbarian Periphery'

Tales of treasure buried in remote locations, and guarded by possessive monsters, are deeply embedded within the folklore of Eurasia. Unearthing such treasures, from kingly swords to life-giving chalices, brings both power and misfortune to ordinary mortals, for they were originally intended as gifts to the gods, or to the spirits of the earth. Archaeologists have often wondered about the sources for such customary narratives, transmitted from past to present by oral rather than written communication. The polymath R. G. Collingwood, for example, viewed folk tales as recollections of earlier forms of social life, disconnected from the material worlds in which they took shape, but nevertheless merging into the historical consciousness of more recent societies.

Such arguments may remain hostage to accusations of romance and speculation. But it is a fact that around the

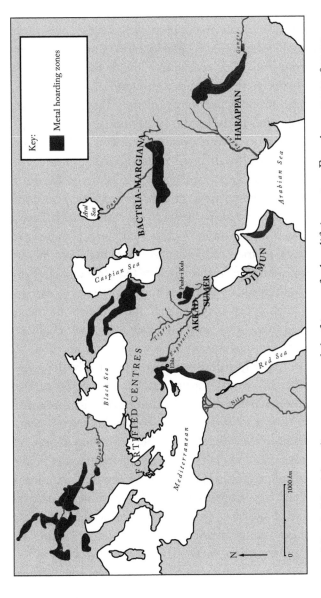

Map 6. Metal-hoarding zones around the fringes of urban life in western Eurasia, c.2500 to 1800 BC

margins of urban trade networks, which took form during the Bronze Age, lies a loosely connected chain of territories in which spectacular hoards of sophisticated metalwork are found, buried mysteriously in the earth, far from major centres of population. We are no longer dealing here with isolated treasure troves, or with exceptional episodes of ceremonial interment, such as those attested in the Royal Tombs at Ur. This is a quite different phenomenon: large quantities of deliberately discarded wealth, distributed across great areas over long periods of time, spanning multiple generations. It was once believed that such concentrations of 'buried treasure' represent the stock-in-trade of itinerant smiths, hidden in times of trouble and never recovered. But the scale and consistency of the phenomenon is too impressive to sustain such ad hoc explanations, and the presence of much finished (and often very fine) metalwork within these deposits also suggests a more complex interpretation.

Two major hoarding zones lie respectively along the Danube, in central Europe, and in the valley of the Ganges in northern India. In Europe the distribution of metal hoards follows the course of major river systems between the Black and Baltic Seas, forming a more or less continuous chain that linked the trade routes along which copper and amber flowed in opposite directions. The hoards often cluster around key points of transit between land- and water-based arteries of movement, and also around restricted paths of access leading to highland sources of metal. Their southernmost distribution lies around the shores of the Black Sea, approaching the northern frontier of the Anatolian trading network (described above) with its commercial sealing devices and standard systems of weight and measure. These European hoards contain both copper and bronze items, including finished tools and weapons, ornamented toggle pins for fastening woollen cloaks, and standard currency bars in the form of neck torques with distinctive looped ends.

In India some hundreds of metal hoards cluster within the once-forested plains between the Ganges and Yamuna rivers (an area known as the *doab*), whose headwaters rise in the western Himalayas, close to the southernmost sources of the Indus. Among those objects consigned to the earth we find extravagantly large versions of weapons such as harpoons and axes, cast in unalloyed copper, including a distinctive type of sword (with an antennae-shaped hilt) also found in such distant regions as northern Afghanistan, the Caucasus, and the Persian Gulf. The northern extremities of the *doab* hoarding zone lie almost precisely at the point where a distinct set of cultural influences begins, looking towards the urban centres of the Indus Valley with their rigidly standardized material cultures, fixed metrological systems, and extensive use of seals to regulate transactions. As in Europe, hoards have usually come to light in the immediate vicinity of important transport routes, such as those leading to the copper sources of Rajasthan via the foothills of the Aravalli Mountains.

In both the European and Indian cases, deposits of metallic wealth are concentrated along river routes leading away from centres of capital accumulation and bulk commerce, but also commanding access to upland zones (along the 'Eurasian metallogenic belt') where minerals of strategic importance to urban economies were concentrated. If we now adjust our focus and zoom in closer towards the nucleus, or rather nuclei, of urban development, we find this pattern replicated with striking regularity. Areas in which metal goods were systematically withdrawn from circulation (more often, now, in collective tombs than hoards) are distributed in a roughly circular formation across the steppe and semi-arid fringes of the Fertile Crescent, usually in close proximity to highland sources of copper and other mineral deposits. They form an inner ring of metal deposition located between the forested hoarding zones of India and Europe, but outside the core areas of urban growth and seal use; a kind of negative imprint around the major centres of population.

We find such metal-rich burials along the highland copper belt of Oman (in the hinterland of *Dilmun*), across the mountains of northern Afghanistan (high above the fortified towns of Turkmenistan), along the steep uplands of the Caucasus and the southern shores of the Black Sea (beyond the urbanized settlements of the Upper Euphrates), in the Pusht-i Kuh Mountains of Luristan (between the urban lowlands of the Diyala Valley and the Susiana plain), and along the coastal plains and adjoining hinterlands of Cilicia, northern Cyprus, and Syria-Lebanon (on the fringes of the Anatolian trade network and the kingdom of Ebla). Each of these areas exhibits distinct burial customs, from the stone tombs of Oman and Luristan to the great earthen mounds (*kurgans*) of the Caucasus, where solid-wheeled wagons pulled by oxen accompanied the dead and their grave goods into the burial chamber. On the Levantine coast bronze axes, daggers, shields, and other warrior gear were dedicated to the gods of the sea, whose temples stood at Byblos and Ugarit. Sacrificial offerings made there also included many decorated toggle pins and bronze neck torques with distinctive looped endings. As has long been recognized, these forms of personal ornamentation find direct parallels in metal hoards along the Danube, far to the north on the other side of the Anatolian Plateau.

'Potlatch' Societies in the History of Eurasia

Contrasts between highland hoarding zones and lowland urban centres have often been seized upon as evidence for deeply rooted cultural, linguistic, or even racial difference. Among the categorical oppositions framed around these contrasts we find 'nomad versus settled', 'tribal versus urban', 'barbarian versus civilized'. Since the late nineteenth century, spectacular burials of metalwork ('hoards') have also been frequently linked to postulated migrations of Indo-European-speaking groups ('hordes'). But such contrasting and symmetrical patterns of wealth consumption are not limited to the Bronze Age. Later examples include the rich tumulus burials of the Scythians, aligned across the margins of the Hellenic world and vividly described by Herodotus;

the distribution of Roman coin hoards along the eastern coastline of the Indian subcontinent (distantly echoed on the Empire's north-west European frontier); and the vast numbers of central Asian *dirhams* recovered from Viking hoards and burials in Scandinavia and northern Russia, where they mark the termini of riverine supply routes that fed slaves and furs to the markets of the Middle East. We are dealing, then, with a phenomenon of extremely long duration in the history of Eurasia.

In seeking alternative explanations, some historians have appealed to comparisons with the *Potlatch* ceremonies conducted by indigenous societies along the Pacific coastline of America and Canada. *Potlatch* was a ritual tournament. Its aim was to secure legal access to intangible rights and privileges such as ranks, titles, and land tenure. The public destruction of particular kinds of wealth, notably woven blankets and sheets of copper, formed an important part of the ritual process. As Marcel Mauss (2002 (1923-4): 47) wrote in *The Gift*:

In a certain number of cases, it is not even a question of giving and returning gifts, but of destroying, so as not to give the slightest hint of desiring your gift to be reciprocated. Whole boxes of olachen (candlefish) oil or whale oil are burnt, as are houses and thousands of blankets. The most valuable copper objects are broken and thrown into the water, in order to put down and 'flatten' one's rival. In this way one not only promotes oneself, but also one's family, up the social scale.

Native American rituals of this kind were observed in recent centuries by European colonists, missionaries, and scholars, and were eventually prohibited under colonial law as wasteful, uncivilized customs. In reality, their expansion—and the incorporation into them of Western trade goods, including money—had a strategic function for local communities confronted by the growing influence of industrial commerce. The economics of sacrifice, to borrow a phrase from Susanne Kuechler (1997), often served the interests of preserving traditional cultural values. Sacrificial rituals involving the destruction of wealth focused upon sensitive resource areas (e.g. mines, forests) and major routes of contact, embedding the movement of people and goods within dense symbolic infrastructures, and forestalling the transformation of these areas into passive supply zones for distant centres of urban consumption. Outside commercial interests were also directly represented and symbolically subverted through the destruction of imported commodities, along with more established symbols of rank.

We might then ask whether similar strategies of resistance were adopted in other parts of the world, in earlier periods of history, and in less overwhelming circumstances than those created by recent European expansion (backed up by large-scale military force and the catastrophic effects of diseases introduced upon local populations)? Mauss in fact assigned ritual systems of the *Potlatch* type a distinct and important place in his comparative history of social contracts. He felt they must once have been 'shared by a very large part of humanity during a very long transitional phase'. Intriguingly, he defined this transitional phase as lying midway between

Neolithic forms of contract, based upon the reciprocal obligations shared by members of a kin group, and the modern world of impersonal contract: 'of the market where money circulates, of sale proper, and above all *of the notion of price reckoned in coinage weighed and stamped with its value*' (original emphasis).

In fact, the circulation of metal in standard units and the use of authorizing stamps to mark commodities were already closely related features of urban economies in Bronze Age Eurasia, long before the invention of formal currencies during the first millennium BC. Coinage simply represents the subdivision of stamped ingots into progressively smaller units, a point often omitted by economic historians who wish to identify the appearance of 'money' (in its familiar material forms) as a major historical turning point. Moreover, the relationship between sacrificial economies (of *Potlatch* type) and the development of economies based on the use of ingot currencies does not conform to Mauss's vision of social evolution. The former did not *develop into* the latter, as he envisioned. Theirs was a relation in space rather than time; one of contiguity rather than succession. Intriguingly, this contiguous growth of sacrificial and urban economies—so integral to the early history of Eurasia— appears quite alien to that of much of the African continent, including the early kingdoms of the Nile Valley. There, instead, we find the ritual management of wealth sacrifice—that is the collective, deliberate, and permanent withdrawing of material goods from circulation—at the very foundation of the urban economy.

1. Gold casing of a cult statue with lapis lazuli inlays around the eyes, from Tell el-Farkha in northern Egypt, *c.*3200 BC ('Late predynastic period').

2. Marble face of a composite figure, with shell and lapis lazuli inlays, from Mari, Syria, c.2500 BC.

3. Monumental stone tower constructed around 9000 BC ('Pre-pottery Neolithic A period') at the site of Jericho (Palestine), preserved to a height of around 9 metres.

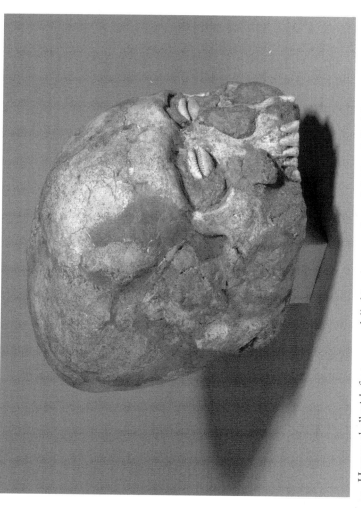

4. Human skull with features modelled in plaster, and eyes inlaid with Red Sea shells, *c.*7500 BC ('Pre-pottery Neolithic B period'; Jericho, Palestine).

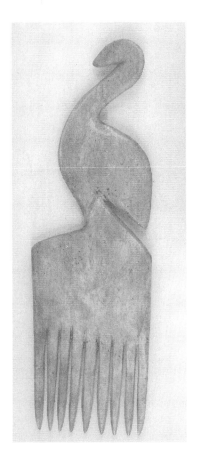

5. Comb with bird ornament, c.3500 BC, from a grave at Ballas in Upper Egypt ('Predynastic period').

6. Ceramic serving vessels of the sixth millennium BC ('Halaf period'), from northern Iraq.

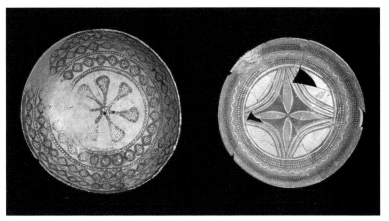

7. Copper sceptres, mace-heads and other ceremonial objects cast in the lost-wax technique, from a hoard discovered at Nahal Mishmar in the Judean Desert (Israel), dating to the late fifth or early fourth millennium BC.

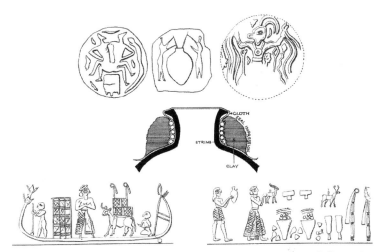

8. Images impressed onto the clay sealings of storage vessels, and illustration of sealing mechanism (above: stamp impressions, late fifth or early fourth millennium BC; below: cylinder impressions, late fourth millennium BC; Mesopotamia and western Iran).

9. Tell Brak (ancient Nagar), in Syria, where urban life dates back to at least 4000 BC. Today its remains still stand over 40 metres above the Upper Khabur plain.

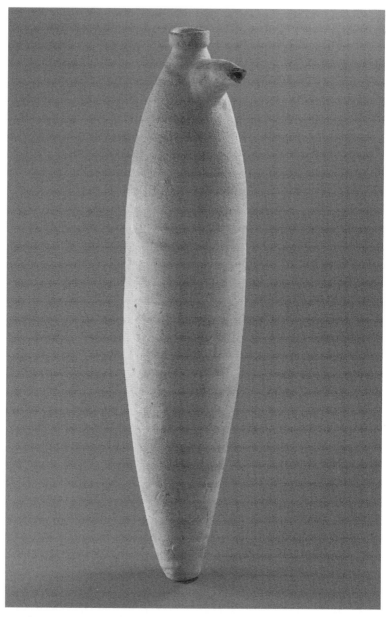

10. Ceramic pouring vessel from the time of the 'Uruk Expansion', c.3200 BC, from Habuba Kabira, Syria.

11. Cosmetic palette inscribed with the name of King Narmer, one of Egypt's earliest rulers, *c*.3100 BC, obverse face.

12. Early cuneiform account (damaged) of bread and beer from the site of Jemdet Nasr, southern Iraq, *c*.3000 BC.

13. Limestone plaque of Ur-Nanshe, ruler of Lagash, c.2500 BC (height, 40 cm). The larger figures show the king, accompanied by close kin and a high official, carrying a basket of mud-bricks for the construction of a temple, and presiding over a banquet to mark its establishment.

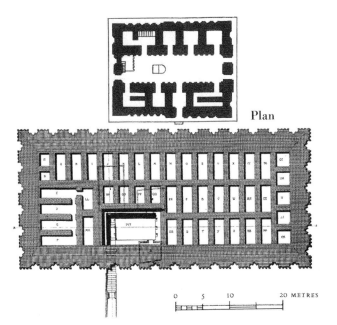

Plan

0   5   10   20 METRES

14. Monumental mud-brick architecture at the end of the fourth millennium BC: the 'White Temple' at Uruk, southern Iraq (above), and an elite tomb at Saqqara, northern Egypt (below).

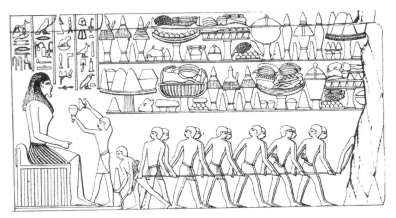

15. Relief carving of a seated statue in transit, receiving an offering of incense, from the tomb of Rashepses at Saqqara, Old Kingdom, c.2400 BC.

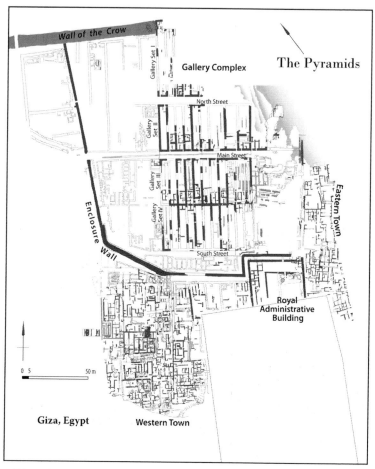

Wall of the Crow

Gallery Set I

Gallery Complex

The Pyramids

North Street

Gallery Set II

Main Street

Gallery Set III

Enclosure Wall

Gallery Set IV

Eastern Town

South Street

Royal Administrative Building

0 5   50 m

Giza, Egypt

Western Town

16. Plan of the workers' settlement near the pyramids of Giza, Old Kingdom, with adjoining towns and fortifications.

17. Syrian bears and vessels arriving in Egypt. Painted limestone relief from the mortuary temple of Sahure at Abusir, *c.*2450 BC.

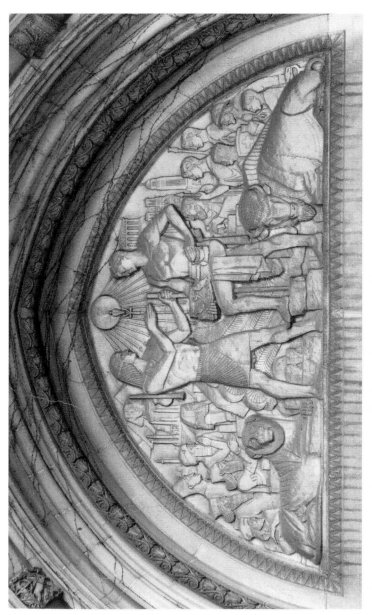

18. Tympanum above the entrance to the Oriental Institute in Chicago.

19. Bronze medallion commemorating the publication of *Description de l'Égypte*, 1826.

20. 'General Napoleon Bonaparte, before the pyramids, contemplates the mummy of a king' (Egyptian Expedition 1798), after the painting by Maurice Orange (1868-1916).

7

COSMOLOGY AND COMMERCE

It should come as no surprise that, in many societies and cultures, gold and silver have been used as money. These are metals which, over the centuries, have been used to adorn the bodies of the gods and the men (and women) in positions of power, and which were of no use in daily life... A money must harbor the presence of the gods.

Maurice Godelier, *The Enigma of the Gift* (1999)

Let the gods eat roasted meat, roasted meat, roasted meat!

Excerpt from a Mesopotamian ritual text (translated by J. Bottéro)

I n his *Ancient Mesopotamia: Portrait of a Dead Civilization* (1964), A. Leo Oppenheim delivered a scathing condemnation of the state of research into divine images and their place in the economic and social life of the ancient Near East. Despite the subsequent appearance of a number of significant studies, his comments remain instructive today:

It is typical of the Assyriologist's culture-conditioned approach to Mesopotamian religion that the role and the function of the divine image in that civilization have never been considered important enough to merit a systematic scholarly investigation. Only as far as the few known statues of gods or goddesses and other representations of the deity have been the concern of the Mesopotamian archaeologist or the historian of art have they received a modicum of the attention they deserve.

Evoking the reflections of Byron's 'Childe Harold', upon seeing the sculptures in the Vatican, Oppenheim went on to attribute this neglect to an 'influence of subconscious associations on the selection of research topics':

The aversion to accepting images as genuine and adequate realisations of the divine presence, manifested in a traditional human form ('the Sun in human limbs array'd') has played an important role in the religious development of the Western world. The roots of the attitude of rejection stem not only from the Judeo-Christian heritage but existed, earlier and independently, in Greek thought. In fact, pro- and anti-iconic tendencies have often been instrumental in shaping trends and releasing events in the history of our culture. And they are far from dead now. They still linger in the scholar's ambivalent attitude toward 'idols' and taint his approach to all alien religions.

Statues of the divine cult, in both Egypt and Mesopotamia, embodied a common set of cultural oppositions. They were sophisticated craft products, the pinnacle of skilled labour conducted in temple and palace workshops. But they could not be represented as merely the outcome of human technology. As countless inscriptions attest, they were composed of 'pure' matter, treated as qualitatively distinct from that of which ordinary commodities were made. Yet the materials required for their manufacture were also *precisely* those which sustained, and were the ardent focus of, commercial transactions: metals, used as currency in international commerce; precious stones and timber traded over great distances via multiple (human) intermediaries.

As Godelier observes, in the citation that opens this chapter, such apparent contradictions reflect universal tendencies governing the relationship between commodities and sacred objects: things made to circulate, and things made to be withheld from circulation. The contrast between these two categories of object is not defined by the use of distinct materials in trade and ritual. Rather it is maintained through contrasting sets of moral and behavioural norms that cause the *same* materials—usually drawn from outside society itself—to move within different spheres of exchange. It is in the process of controlling the flow of these particular materials (metals being a prime example) that the parallel worlds of sacred and profane transactions are constituted and kept apart:

Once again, let us note that, if a currency is to circulate as a medium of payment or as wealth, it must be authorized, as it were, by its ties with some reality which does not circulate, which is kept out of the exchange sphere and which appears as the true source of their exchange-value.

Both in Egypt and in Mesopotamia the ritual feeding of the gods via their statue bodies also demanded the admixture—to roasted animal parts and other food offerings—of fragrant incense, derived from tree resins brought from distant lands, such as southern Arabia and the high forests of Syria and Lebanon. The wood and sap of odoriferous trees—myrrh, frankincense, pine, cedar, juniper, terebinth—were essential in attracting the gods to take up residence of their local shrines. But these substances too could be procured only through long-range commerce with the world beyond the alluvial plains of the Nile and Tigris–Euphrates. For all of these reasons, cult statues and the rituals surrounding them provide a privileged point of entry to the main theme of this chapter: the fragile relationship between commodities and the sacred.

Flesh of the Gods

With Oppenheim's words in mind, it is instructive to consider which specific attributes of ancient Near Eastern cult statues attracted the scorn of the Old Testament prophets:

For the customs of the people are false. He cuts a tree from the forest, the work of the hands of a craftsman, with a chisel. He decorates it with silver and gold; with nails and hammers they set them firmly in place so they don't topple over. Their idols are beaten gold, and they cannot speak; they have to be carried, for they cannot walk. Be not afraid of them, for they cannot do evil, neither is it in them to do good.... (After all) it is only wood. Hammered silver is imported from Tarshish, and gold from Ophir. They are the work of the craftsman and of the hands of the goldsmith; their clothing is violet and purple; they are all the work of skilled men . . . there is no breath in them.   (Jeremiah 10: 3–15)

The emphasis of this parody is revealing. Throughout, there is an implied contrast with the unity of mind and deed that characterizes the creative acts of Yahweh: pure in nature, swift and unwavering of execution. Instead, the disunity of the group whose labours contribute to the fashioning of a divine cult image is stressed. The laboriousness and uncertainty of the process is highlighted, as is the constant reliance on artifice and man-made tools to produce special effects. The mundane provenance of the precious materials used is also emphasized. Their sources can be precisely named: Tarshish (in Iberia) and Ophir (in Arabia). These regions lay within the compass of worldly commerce during the Iron Age. They were part of profane, not sacred topography.

Now let us contrast this passage with a much earlier one, taken from the Sumerian poem known as *Inanna's Descent to the Underworld*, a distant precursor to the Greek myth telling of Persephone's abduction by Hades. Drawn unwisely to enter the gates of the Underworld, where the dead dwell, Inanna—represented as a cult statue throughout the composition—is herself condemned to death. Her descent from the realm of immortals into that of mortals is symbolized by a transformation in the nature of her flesh, from an array of precious stones and metals (the flesh of the gods) into a rotting haunch of meat (the flesh of mortals), which the rulers of the Underworld hang on a peg in the wall. Her handmaiden Ninshubur pleads for assistance to Enlil, the divine father of Inanna, in whose own words she addresses him:

> Father Enlil, let not your daughter be put to death in the Netherworld,
> Let not your good metal be covered with the dust of the Netherworld,
> Let not your good lapis lazuli be broken up into the stone of the stoneworker.
> Let not your boxwood be cut up into the wood of the woodworker.
>
> (After Kramer 1961)

Here the death of Inanna's divine body is poetically described as a process of commoditization. Ninshubur conveys the corruption of her divine flesh, its loss of 'goodness' (i.e. purity), through exposure to the hands of ordinary craftsmen. Once integral to her identity, the components of Inanna's cult statue now face the dismal prospect of being reduced to the status of anonymous goods. The metaphor is chosen to reflect the fact that commodities belong to the world of humans who, unlike gods, must suffer death and destruction. They carry with them the polluting influence of mortality, signified by the decaying meat into which Inanna is transformed in the subterranean world of the dead. Upon her eventual release from the Underworld, the meat is revivified by the application of sacred, cleansing substances: 'the grass of life' and 'the water of life'.

Both Mesopotamian and Egyptian sources concur in their description of cult statues as being *born* rather than made. Just like newborns they were washed and surrounded with cleansing liquids and fragrances, before taking up residence in their shrines. Substances comprising their skin, flesh, bones, and hair arise directly into their bodies from sources beyond the reach of mortals. These materials are described as virgin matter, pure because they are unworked by human hands, sacred because they transcend those properties of number that make profane goods subject to ordinary principles of quantification. The metals, stones, and timber in question are exalted as the creations of mountains whose peaks pierce the heavens, and of trees whose roots penetrate the crust of the earth. They are counted only in mystical units of number, charged with esoteric meanings, or in volumes that exceed the range of the possible. In similar measure they surpass the temporal scope of human affairs. Just as their space is the magnified space of divine action, so their time is the deep time of cosmic creation evoked through ritual incantations and performances. The statue, as Victor Hurowitz (2006: 13) observes, is 'a concentrate of a god which fills the universe, packaged in a form which can be conveniently introduced and worshipped in a temple'. To treat it as a subject of human technology, or reduce its materials to the status of commodities, is quite simply to end its 'life'.

Such 'putting to death' under hammer, chisel, and fire cannot have been uncommon. Written and pictorial sources from Egypt and Mesopotamia testify to the continuous manufacture of divine cult statues over a period of millennia. Yet almost none are preserved from either region. This can be attributed in part to their materials of construction. Aside from precious stones, these were typically perishable (fine woods and textile garments) or recyclable (metals). A rare survivor, recovered from the foundations of the temple of Horus at Hierakonpolis in Upper Egypt, confirms the impression given by written sources. Its wooden core—evoking the temple's principal deity as a crowned falcon—has rotted away. But its shape is preserved in negative by the sheets of gold and pure (unalloyed) copper that once enclosed it; and its eyes, formed by a rod of obsidian passing through hollows in the head, retain their jet black stare. This lonely exception serves only to prove the rule that the 'lives' of cult statues generally ended in dismemberment and recycling, rather than wholesale consecration to the ground.

Matters of Origin

To further grasp the relationship between cult statues and the world of commodities, we first need to understand more about the nature of the distance between mortals and the gods, as ordained at the beginning of time, and the special role of exotic substances in manifesting and overcoming that distance. Mesopotamian narratives of how the world came into being are preserved mainly in cuneiform compositions dating to the early second millennium BC, or later. But they share certain consistent premises regarding the nature of human and divine bodies, premises that undoubtedly rest upon older foundations. A number of these myths, including *Atrahasis*—the familiar story of a wise man who survives a great flood by building an ark—commence in similar fashion, with the primeval gods who personify elemental forces: sky, air, fresh water, salt water, and fluvial mud. It is they, we are told, who dug out the beds of the Tigris and Euphrates at the dawn of time, and who maintained canals (the 'lifelines of the land') to irrigate the great marshes and provide themselves with food. To lighten this terrible burden, the great gods procreate and make lesser gods to labour in their place. But the new generation of gods rebels, and their noisy objections form the pretext for the creation of humans, whose destiny is to 'bear the load of the gods' and supply them with offerings of food and drink.

According to Mesopotamian mythology, the first humans were shaped from a specific mixture of substances. The gods slew one of their own number and, by mixing his flesh and blood with clay, created the raw material out of which mortal bodies were fashioned. It is the mixing of these substances that initiates both the provisioning of the gods by humans and the construction of their first earthly dwellings, which are made from the same distinctive blend of materials. In *Atrahasis* this episode occurs near the beginning of the story. In the house of the 'womb deities' the mixture of clay and blood is softened by treading. Then it is given the forms of seven males and seven females. Between them is placed a mud-brick rendered from the same mix of materials, which brings divine blessings and protection upon the house of their gestation and birth. Armed with picks and spades, the newly created humans set to work, producing a surplus of food to sustain both themselves and the gods, and multiplying at such a rate that the latter—disturbed by their clamour—send down natural disasters from heaven to curb their numbers.

The provision of food to the gods is thereby placed at the centre of human existence, as its literal *raison d'être*. In the later narrative known as the *Epic of Creation*, the place of the king in this process is addressed through the heroic figure of Marduk, a god who assumes the titles and responsibilities of rulership. Having quelled an uprising against the higher gods, Marduk uses the blood of his slain foe Qingu (no admixture of clay is mentioned this time) to make humans, so that his fellow gods will have leisure. In gratitude the gods set to work for a year, forming mud-bricks to build Marduk's royal city of Babylon as a shrine in which they may dwell.

Egyptian notions of life and its genesis, expressed in ritual texts of the Old Kingdom, make no explicit refer-ence to the creation of human beings (although the lived experience of the human body is their ontological point of departure). Nor, in Egyptian cosmology, does newly formed life require a house (mud-brick or otherwise) to dwell in. The inception of the cosmos is imagined rather as a flow of substances between divine bodies. Creation begins with a formless mass, into which Atum—the initiator of the cosmos—injects new materials from his own body by masturbating, sneezing, or spitting. All of these materials are fluids (semen, mucus, saliva), by-products of bodily processes that are only partially controllable (the need to achieve sexual climax, or to expel pollutants). Their escape from the body takes the form of an undirected projection or ejaculation. The generation of the Egyptian cosmos thus involves two interrelated processes: the semi-voluntary injection of diverse substances into the homogeneity of primordial matter, and a corresponding loss of potency from the Creator's body. This potency flows into a series of sub-bodies, which take form from his various emissions. And these sub-bodies are hierarchically ranked, from the lesser gods of the Ennead down through their offspring (including Isis and Osiris) to Horus, the deity whose earthly body is inhabited by living kings.

The creative acts of the Egyptian gods differ from those of humans in a variety of ways. Ritual texts repeatedly emphasize that the gods fashion their own bodies and generate their own life force. In his godlike aspect, the king similarly 'begets himself on his own mother'. Unlike the procreative acts of Mesopotamian gods, which involved an exchange of semen, this self-fashioning is not the result of a transfer of substances between separate, bounded individuals. Rather it is a fluid merging of boundless forces, which are in constant flux, like the shifting motion of rivers or stars which share the same properties of movement, and in which mortals can dimly perceive the gods' presence. Egypt's gods were thereby distinguished from mortals, who must exchange in order to procreate, and also from the dead, whose survival beyond the grave was contingent upon a constant flow of sacrificial gifts.

Contact between humanity and the gods was nevertheless possible, because one of them had miraculously descended to earth in the form of the king. His bodily presence made manifest the primordial rupture in the fabric of the universe, the original escape of divine substances from the higher to the lower orders of existence. In Egyptian mythology this vertical flow of sacred power is not represented as a chronological succession. It does not constitute the replacement of one kind of world (the sacred one) by another (the profane one). Rather the primal unity of creation survives alongside the newly made cosmos, in a fragmented or potential form: a state of continuous coming-into-being. It is the designated role of the king to sustain this fragile balance of forces, by controlling the movement of pure and polluting substances from one order of existence to another. It is he who must offer sacrifices to tempt the gods, attracting them to feed via their statue bodies, so that some residue of sacred power can be trapped on earth and redistributed among his subjects, both the living and the exalted dead.

The Mechanics of Sacrifice

While the perpetual hunger of the Egyptian and Mesopotamian gods arose from quite different causes, we can nevertheless point to significant similarities in their manner of feeding. As a vital prelude to the commence-ment of food offerings, cult statues had to undergo a rite of initiation that was known by the same name in both countries: the 'Opening of the Mouth'. Its execution was far from identical, and each developed a distinct body of literary and ritual exegesis around it. Yet underlying commonalities remain in the physical procedures used to bring the gods closer to humanity: the choice of exotic materials for the body of the statue, including specific details of physiognomy (Chapter 2); the selection of substances to be heated or poured in its vicinity; and the magical techniques used to animate its flesh and purify its surroundings. Among those techniques we find the burning of incense, the use of spouted vessels to shoot a stream of libations over the statue, and the sacrificial slaughter of animals to the accompaniment of music, dance, and acrobatics.

The gods of both countries fed upon the smoke rising from braziers, on which were roasted a mixture of meat, cereal, and vegetable dishes, infused with the scent of incense. Their ingestion of these foods, which may have been initiated by passing them before the eyes of the cult statue, was most likely indicated by organic transforma-tions in the food itself, which took place during the process of cooking: the dissipation of liquids and the escape of fumes from the roast. Both the Egyptian and Mesopotamian gods rejected the meaty parts of animal offerings, which were boiled, stewed, or dried in a secondary process that readied them for human commerce and consumption (hence it is not uncommon for archaeologists to recover cattle horns, hooves, and de-fleshed bones in the vicinity of places where sacred offerings were made). Bread and beer, warmed by the sacrificial meat and impregnated with its juices and smells, were also recycled among the living community, and temples in both regions were equipped with extensive facilities for the processing, brewing, and baking of cereal products. The bureaucratic classification and ranking of comestibles—which can be traced back to the beginnings of urban life (Chapter 5)—is best understood as an extension of these exclusionary rituals, in which the highest tier of produce was always set aside for the nourishment of the gods, and for the select community of ritual actors who consumed the consecrated residues of sacred offerings.

Offering rituals implied a change of state not only for the statue, but also for the group engaged in feeding it. Here our pictorial and written sources are undoubtedly misleading. They are stylized representations, in which the sacrificial process is reduced to static gestures and formulaic recitations. In reality, the secluded environment around the cult statue must have been saturated with exotic aromas, sounds, and fluids. Surviving depictions convey little of this visceral messiness, or of the contagious excitement of ritual killing that accompanied the sacrifice of animals. Shared ingestion of a cumulative flow of consecrated substances—blood, water, beer, unguents, but also solids such as meat and bread, all of them enveloped by the spread of scented fumes—must nevertheless have been essential in binding together a ritual community around the statue, which would thereafter share in the responsibility of its care. In other contexts, the same procedures were followed for the ritual inauguration of statues devoted to kings and ancestors, with similarly cohesive effects for the group involved.

The Two Faces of Bronze Age 'Trade'

It was through contact with their gods that the societies of Egypt and Mesopotamia expressed their sense of ancestry and belonging, their particular modes of attachment to land, locality, and place. Yet the earthly bodies of the Egyptian and Mesopotamian gods were made of similar materials—exotic to both regions—and were nourished in common ways. Commerce and cosmology, the interregional conduct of 'trade' and the local performance of 'ritual', cannot then be logically separated. Matters of origin and matters of exchange were interwoven, both literally and metaphorically. One brought the other into existence, such that ritual celebration of the local moral order contained within it a veiled reference to forces and processes that transcended it in time and space, that subverted it and exposed it to failure at its very point of performance. Only in myth, in the imagination of a world populated solely by gods, could this paradox be overcome. It is the gods alone who, we are told, created life out of raw clay, blood, semen, and saliva—base materials of limitless quantity—without first adding to them those rare and purifying substances that bridged the distance between heaven and earth. Mortals, and sacred kings who dwelled temporarily upon the earth, faced a more fraught and circuitous journey to the divine.

8

THE LABOURS OF KINGSHIP

> When the gods instead of man
> Did the work, bore the loads,
> The gods' load was too great,
> The work too hard, the trouble too much.
>
> > Opening lines of *Atrahasis*, the
> > Mesopotamian Flood Myth
> > (second millennium BC,
> > translated by S. Dalley)

Among the less well-known studies of Sumerian kingship is that written by Kaiser Wilhelm II, the last Emperor of Germany between 1888 and 1918. Deposed from the baroque palaces of Prussia upon the declaration of the Weimar Republic, the Kaiser spent his final years in the small manor house of Doorn, in the Dutch province of Utrecht. There he divided his time between writing and felling great trees, kingly labours which he could, and did, trace back to the legendary Gilgamesh of Uruk. In *Das Königtum im alten Mesopo-tamien* (1938) he wrote with pathos of the unbroken line reaching back across the millennia from the German emperors to the first kings of Sumer, a line of sacral kingship demonstrated—or so he imagined—by the cosmic symbols on the Kaiser's robe of office. Stripped of political and economic power, the last German emperor had come to an important realization. The true power of kingship, and his only hope of a return to glory, lay buried deep in the prehistory of kingship itself and, more particularly, in recapturing the monarch's original role as mediator between a frail and fragmented humanity and the mysterious totality of the supernatural. But ascendant forces of liberalism overshadowed the Kaiser's hopes for a neo-Sumerian revival in central Europe, and the fascist form of imperialism that followed the Republic extended the old dynastic obsession with bloodlines and heredity to the body politic at large. The last Kaiser died a modest death at Doorn, with soldiers of the Third Reich standing guard at his gates.

In the concluding chapters of this book, I return to the curious relationship between the end of the Old Regime in Europe and the Western rediscovery of the ancient Near East. Here, however, I remain focused upon the birth of what Benedict Anderson, in his *Imagined Communities* (1983), calls 'the dynastic realm':

These days it is perhaps difficult to put oneself empathetically into a world in which the dynastic realm appeared for most men as the only imaginable 'political' system. For in fundamental ways 'serious' monarchy lies transverse to all modern conceptions of political life. Kingship orders everything around a high centre. Its legitimacy derives from divinity, not from populations, who, after all, are subjects, not citizens.

126

In its essentials, Anderson's broad definition might apply equally well to dynastic societies of the Early Bronze Age or the early twentieth century AD. It captures the extraordinary longevity of monarchic institutions in world history, the 'persistence of the old regime', as Arno Mayer impatiently puts it. But beneath the surface similarities, we find constant variation in the forms taken by kingship, and by the relationships between kings, gods, and subjects.

The Dynastic Realm

As Henri Frankfort observed in his *Kingship and the Gods* (1948) sacral kingship was, from its very beginnings, Janus-faced. Mesopotamian rulers—contrary to the idealism of the Sumerian King List—were typically one among many, distributed across a divided political landscape comprising independent city-states, which vied for land and resources but nonetheless recognized a common religious bond. They rarely exercised power without divine sanction, but—as Irene Winter (2008: 80) observes—they were not 'ontologically defined as divine'. Their proximity to the gods was always a fleeting and tenuous affair. The Egyptian king was a different matter. Not only was he the sole protector of the Two Lands. He was himself a visible god, an embodiment of Horus, although his ability to interact on an equal footing with the other gods was only fully realized after his death and departure from the earthly realm.

Royal power, then, assumed strikingly different forms in Egypt and Mesopotamia, giving rise to further hybrids and mixtures on their margins, where societies of smaller scale were drawn to produce their own, local variants of the dynastic realm. By 2500 BC kingdoms of varying shapes and sizes extended from the Nile Valley to the maritime cities of Lebanon, across the Syrian Saddle (dominated by the palace of Ebla), and down through the city-states of the Mesopotamian alluvium towards the highland monarchies of western Iran (Elam and Awan). The political make-up of urban societies to the south and east—those of the Iranian Plateau, the Persian Gulf, the Indus Valley, and Central Asia—remains unclear, owing partly to a lack of written sources. Egypt and Byblos were partners at the highest level of diplomatic contact, and gifts from the Egyptian court (filtered through coastal intermediaries) reached as far inland as Ebla, whose rulers conducted diplomacy with smaller polities along the northern Mesopotamian steppe. The latter's sphere of contact merged, in turn, with that of city-states to the south, on the Sumerian plain. We are confronted, then, by loosely integrated circuits of interdynastic exchange, rather than a fully integrated and self-conscious system spanning the distance from Egypt to Mesopotamia, of the kind attested much later in the 'Amarna Letters of the fourteenth century BC. The commercial underpinnings of these relationships are immediately apparent in the spatial distribution of palace-centred societies. Pharaoh's court at Memphis (the meeting point of the

Nile Valley and delta), the reception halls and ancestral tombs of the Syrian caravan kings, and the great urban households of the Sumerian dynasts: all sat possessively astride the main overland and maritime routes of their day.

How should we explain the differences between Egyptian and Mesopotamian concepts of sacral kingship? Neither region has left us a written tradition of constitutional law. As Bruce Wells (2005) observes, their texts were 'not the repositories of law, merely the reflections of it'. The duties and limitations of royal power, as I go on to describe, were encoded and enforced in other ways, 'inscribed' within the ritual activities undertaken by kings to ensure communication between the visible world and the hidden domain of the gods. The so-called Mesopotamian 'law codes'—including the famous Code of Hammurabi (c.1750 BC), now in the Louvre Museum of Paris—are best understood as rhetorical expressions of these duties. As has often been noted, these inscriptions seem divorced from the realities of legislation, and—despite their listing of specific crimes and punishments—are almost never cited in contemporaneous records of actual legal proceedings. Rather they appear to be formalized presentations of royal virtue to the literate elite, to posterity, and above all to the gods. It was after all the gods, and not the proximate world of human affairs, that provided blessings and offered the ultimate sanction on the exercise of power. The right of kings to judge and administer human affairs on earth was grounded in the duties they performed, and the services they rendered to the gods.

Jan Assmann (2001) has identified three principal levels of contact with the divine in the ancient Near East. These he terms *cultic* (acts performed for or on behalf of the gods), *cosmic* (an awareness of the gods as distant and unbounded forces), and *mythical* (an attempt to know and approach them through narrative). Each holds implications for our understanding of the relationship between local forms of power and trans-local patterns of exchange. Of the three levels identified by Assmann, however, it is the cultic dimension of religious experience that I focus on in the remainder of this chapter; i.e. evidence for and representations of the physical points of contact through which communication with the gods occurred, and by means of which binding relationships were forged with them. A comparison of Egypt and Mesopotamia, in this regard, reveals consistent differences between the types of activities customarily used to express communion between kings and gods, differences which reach back to the prehistoric past (Chapter 3), and are most clearly apprehended when we place the evidence from one region in the perspective of the other. I will deal first with the ritual labours demanded of Mesopotamian kings, before going on to consider the wider background to the emergence of the Egyptian Old Kingdom, and the distinct place of Pharaoh as a mediator between the living, the dead, and the gods.

Mesopotamia: The Cohabitation of Gods and Mortals

In his *The Tower of Babel* (1563), Pieter Breughel the Elder portrayed the building activities of a Babylonian king. In the foreground of his painting, craftsmen have left their labours to grovel at the feet of the monarch, who proceeds through the bustling scene in full regalia, wielding a rod of command. There are no gods in the bright blue skies above Breughel's tower; only clouds. This image of royal hubris from the European Renaissance forms an instructive contrast with those (unknown of course to Breughel) produced in ancient Mesopotamia to commemorate royal building projects. Among the earliest known are a series of stone plaques carved for Ur-Nanshe, king of Lagash and founder of its first dynasty (*c.*2500 BC), which combine picture and text to present him as the ideal builder of temples for the gods. On two of these monuments it is recorded that he sent out 'ships of Dilmun' to acquire timber from 'foreign lands'. The pictorial scenes juxtapose images of Ur-Nanshe seated, with a cup, before his wife and children (a scribe and snake-charmer are also named), and carrying a basket on his head.

In later written sources, the carrying of the basket is associated with the king's ceremonial role in forming and laying the first mud-brick of a new temple. He is characteristically represented, not as a lofty overseer, but as an active participant in the building process, carrying tools, and holding aloft the basket of clay from which bricks are fashioned. The physicality of the king's participation is constantly stressed through detailed and ponderous references to the techniques of construction: the mixing of mortar—to which he adds special substances such as the cuttings of aromatic plants, cedar resin, perfumed oils, unguents, honey, and ghee—and the careful forming of the first mud-brick in a mould made from exotic wood. A carved stone monument (or 'stele') uncovered within the sacred precinct of Ur shows the gods walking directly before the figure of one such labouring king (probably Ur-Namma, founder of the city's third dynasty, c.2100 BC), guiding his activities and receiving his offerings of libations. On the reverse side we find celebratory scenes of music, wrestling, and animal sacrifice, to mark the consecration of the god's new dwelling.

The temple-building activities of Mesopotamian kings were commemorated, not merely as spectacular technical achievements, but also as solemn rites of passage, during which a mere mortal became, for a brief period of time, an instrument of divine intelligence. A hymn composed for Gudea, a ruler of Lagash in the late third millennium BC, narrates his renovation of Eninnu, the House of Ningirsu, patron deity of the city. It begins with a nocturnal encounter between king and god, in which—as Richard Averbeck (2003) puts it—the king must 'virtually prise the specific desires and plans for the temple out of the heart of the deity for whom the temple was to be built'. Only once in possession of this knowledge:

He raised the brand-new carrying basket and set it
before the mould.
Gudea put the clay in the mould, acted precisely as
prescribed, and he
Succeeded in making a most beautiful brick for the
House.
(Excerpt from the Temple Hymn of Gudea,
Cylinder A; after Edzard 1997)

Each subsequent phase of construction draws king and
god closer together, culminating in a feast—literally a
'housewarming party'—to welcome Ningirsu and his
divine consort Bau into their new home. A significant
portion of the text describes, at greater length than can
be conveyed here, the gathering in of building materials
from beyond the alluvium. The king's construction of
the temple has the effect of a mighty whirlwind, compelling resources—extracted by gods and carried by the
peoples of foreign lands—towards its centre:

The Elamites came to him from Elam, the Susians came to
him from Susa. Magan and Meluha loaded wood from their
mountains upon their shoulders for him, and to build the
house of Ningirsu, they gathered for Gudea at his city Girsu.

We read how Ningirsu directs Gudea to the 'impene-
trable mountains' of cedar and stone, and of the arrival
of ships loaded with gravel, gypsum, and bitumen.
'Translucent carnelian' is summoned to him from
Meluha, and precious metals—gold, silver, and copper—
descend from their highland sources as offerings to 'the
man in charge of building his master's house'.

On completion of his task, the king works together with the gods to prepare the house for Ningirsu's arrival, fumigating it with incense, purifying its foundations by sprinkling them with precious oil, and marking the corners with a paste into which he first mixes carnelian and lapis lazuli. These portions of the text find corroboration in the excavated remains of Mesopotamian temples. As Henri Frankfort (1942) discovered during his fieldwork in the Diyala Valley of eastern Iraq, temple foundations were laid upon raised platforms filled with clean sand: 'to accentuate the structure, to mark out its sacred site as distinct from the profane soil which is subject to the accidents of daily life, being tilled at one time, made to accommodate a dwelling at another, transformed into a cemetery at yet another period'. Buried within the corners of these platforms were small, functionless pieces of gold, copper, carnelian, lapis lazuli, and other materials originating far outside the alluvium. Copper pegs, topped by images of deities, have been similarly recovered from temple foundations, echoing Gudea's divine injunction to drive the foundation pegs of the city god into the sanctified ground, so that the fields and flocks of Lagash may flourish.

Excavation has also revealed the remains of mudbrick altars on which offerings were spilled or burned before the cult images of the gods. By contrast with Egypt, where incense was offered from portable containers or on mobile stands, Mesopotamian altars were fixed points of communication with the divine, built into the inner sanctum of the temple or located in its central courtyard. A thick coat of plaster sealed their surfaces, preventing the absorption of fluids into the brickwork. And watertight grooves (lined with bitumen) were installed to guide any surplus liquids down into vessels, placed below the altar to capture their flow. Libations passing over the altar, but not consumed by the gods, were thus recycled for other purposes. As consecrated substances they could be mixed with base materials such as clay and fashioned into portable cult figures, or fed to the ancestors via terracotta pipes, specially installed in their tombs to carry such fluids down to the Underworld.

Divine attention could also be attracted from above, by the roasting of meat on outdoor altars. Jean Bottéro (2004) has commented on the intriguing absence of roasted and grilled meats from profane cooking recipes, preserved among the royal archives of later periods. He further notes the frequent occurrence of these foods in liturgical texts, which describe the presentation of roasted animal parts to the gods on dishes of precious metal. Literary sources describe how the gods converge 'like flies' around the aromatic fumes of burning meats as they rise high into the air, flavoured with the smoke of incense. Bottéro's explanation of this practice as an 'archaic' survival from prehistoric times contains an important kernel of truth (Chapter 3). But in dismissing its retention as an example of religious conservatism he misses the particular significance of meat-roasting as a technical act, reserved for those special occasions when mortals sought to overcome the distance between their own plane of existence and that of the gods.

The effectiveness ascribed to this act of communion is revealed, albeit obliquely, in a passage towards the end of Gudea's temple hymn, which celebrates the banquet presented to the gods in their new home: 'Syrup, ghee, wine, sour milk, *gipar* fruit, fig-cakes topped with cheese, dates,... and small grapes, things untouched by fire, were the foods for the gods which he prepared with syrup and ghee.' Why, on this most auspicious of occasions, are the foods in question singled out as being 'untouched by fire', if not to acknowledge that for a short time, circumscribed by the consecration of their earthly dwellings, the gods and their mortal servant shared a common plane of commensality?

Old Kingdom Egypt: Mesopotamia's Neighbour in Africa

Towards the end of the fourth millennium BC, the communities of the Nile Valley and Delta coalesced to form a single royal domain. The process of political fusion unfolded under the stimulus of close interaction with neighbouring societies along the Levantine seaboard. For the first time, donkey caravans plied the land bridge across the Mediterranean shoreline of the Sinai Peninsula. And the inception of sail-powered navigation in the eastern Mediterranean increased the scope of maritime trade between the Nile Delta and the ports of Canaan. Intriguingly, however, the earliest reliably dated depiction of a sailing vessel in this part of the world originates to the south of Egypt, in the burial of a local chieftain at Qustul, in northern Sudan. Both its southerly location and its execution on a stone vessel used for burning incense point towards maritime trade in the Red Sea basin, further demonstrated by the presence in Egyptian burials of obsidian from sources around the Horn of Africa. Much still remains to be discovered about this early Red Sea trade, and its wider implications for the movement of goods and ideas between Egypt and Sumer.

Among the technologies absorbed by Egypt from western Asia in the centuries preceding political unification we find new modes of farming (plough agriculture, dairy production, viticulture), commercial techniques (use of cylinder seals to mark royal produce), dietary practices, and forms of cuisine (notably the centralized production of leavened bread and beer). Less tangible imports are suggested by the appearance of monsters from the Mesopotamian bestiary on some of Egypt's earliest royal monuments, including the famous cosmetic palette of King Narmer (*c.*3100 BC), where a pair of serpent-necked lions frames the depression used for grinding pigments. As David O'Connor (2002) suggests, the minerals ground on ceremonial cosmetic palettes may have been used in the consecration of cult statues. Further traces of Mesopotamian influence have long been noted in the forms taken by Egypt's earliest examples of monumental architecture. Made of mud-brick rather than stone, they comprised massive rectangular tombs and enclosures for the performance of the king's mortuary cult. During the First Dynasty (*c.*2900–2800 BC) these imposing structures appear in varying combinations at important administrative centres throughout the country, with notable concentrations at Abydos (in the south) and Saqqara (in the north). All share a distinctive type of facade, formed by regularly spaced sequences of alternating niches and buttresses. The same variegated facades ornamented the exterior walls of early temples in Mesopotamia, where their use in demarcating sacred buildings can be traced back at least to the fifth millennium BC.

On early Egyptian tombs, external recesses in the brickwork were brightly painted with mesmerizing depictions of hanging textiles, giving an illusion of permeability to a monument that was, in reality, solid and impermeable. Once endowed with material offerings, which filled the internal chambers of the tomb and surrounded the mummified body and its cult statues, the entire structure was permanently sealed and rendered inaccessible to human visitors. The presence of surface images that imply the opposite becomes less enigmatic when we realize that the painted niches formed a backdrop for the performance of sacrifices, which involved the burning of substances (incense and select animal parts) that gave off copious amounts of smoke. Entangled within the patterned exterior of the tomb, mingling with and animating its decorated surface, the movement of these intangible fumes blurred the boundaries separating the outside from the inside, and those without from the hungry recipients within. The overall point becomes clearer still when we note that, by Old Kingdom times, these elaborate 'false doors' had migrated to the internal chambers of the tomb (by this time built of stone rather than mud-brick), marking out the point of ritual communion where the living made offerings to the deceased.

Given the existence of other similarities between the ritual treatment of cult statues in Egypt and Mesopotamia, it is not inconceivable that certain core ideas and practices relating to their use passed between these areas during the later part of the fourth millennium BC. The selective nature of such adoptions—tin-bronze, olive cultivation, wheeled vehicles, and the rearing of woolly sheep were among the technologies initially rejected—indicates that the process of borrowing was strongly directed by the internal requirements of emergent elites within Egypt itself. Moreover, all that was borrowed was transformed in the process, such that (from a technical point of view) the resemblances between Egypt and Mesopotamia always appear imprecise. Their specific *ways* of preparing fields, baking bread, brewing beer, marking commodities, forming and laying mud-bricks, and nourishing the gods are indirect reflections of one another, characterized by both underlying similarities (common principles) and subtle differences of execution.

With the consolidation of the dynastic realm, around 3000 BC, the Egyptian court—with its capital at Memphis, near modern Cairo—set about redefining its interactions with the outside world. An open frontier was established to the gold mines of the Nubian Desert, and a rival polity in the vicinity of Qustul was eliminated in the process. Movement was restricted along the land route to Asia, and the mineral resources of the Sinai Peninsula were brought under royal control. The court also sought to monopolize maritime traffic in the eastern Mediterranean and the Red Sea through a variety of cultural strategies, which targeted both foreign and domestic audiences. They included the pursuit of diplomatic relations with foreign chiefs; the foundation of temples for the Egyptian goddess Hathor in distant locations such as Byblos (and perhaps also *Punt*); and the theatrical 'staging' of long-distance trade in locally significant ceremonies, which I discuss further below.

By the Fourth Dynasty, the focus of royal building projects had shifted decisively to the low desert around the capital at Memphis. At Saqqara, Dahshur, Abu Rawash, and on the Giza Plateau, monumental pyramids and adjoining temples were built in quick succession to house the royal mortuary cults. The design of these precocious structures was grounded in architectural innovations of the preceding dynasty, which saw the first use of stone on a monumental scale, most strikingly in the step pyramids of Djoser and his successors. In addition to vast quantities of limestone, quarried from mines along the margins of the floodplain, the construction of pyramids and their associated temples required the use of exotic materials such as pink granite (from Aswan), gneiss (from the Western Desert), and large quantities of cedar (imported by ship from Lebanon). High quality foreign timber was used for both tomb and temple fittings, and also for the ceremonial barges buried alongside the Great Pyramid of Khufu at Giza, which have antecedents extending back to the First Dynasty near the earlier royal cemetery at Abydos.

Royal mortuary cults were endowed with agricultural estates that continued to function long after the completion of the tomb and its associated structures. The official function of these land allotments was to supply ongoing offerings for the statue cult of the tomb-owner. As well as livestock and farming equipment, each such estate comprised teams of dependent labourers, craft specialists, priests, and scribes. While many of these endowments were under the control of the royal family, others were granted to private individuals distributed throughout the country. In this way, spaces occupied by the royal and elite dead gradually became the foundation of an extensive administrative network, which increasingly dominated the productive economy of the living.

The growth of royal funerary cults also gave rise to a new form of urban life, entirely without parallel in Mesopotamia. 'Pyramid towns', as they have come to be known, were centrally administered settlements of considerable scale, established adjacent to the royal tombs and mortuary temples they served, and after which they were named. The layout of one such town on the Giza Plateau, associated with the great pyramids of the Fourth Dynasty, has been reconstructed in some detail. Its high boundary walls surround a rigidly orthogonal street-plan. Central facilities were present for administration, food production (beer brewing and baking), sleeping, and other mundane activities. Such a totalizing scheme for communal life was not designed to foster the growth of a permanent population. It was geared, rather, towards the rapid socialization of incoming groups, who took up residence there for part of the year to provide skilled labour for monumental construction projects, or to otherwise serve the royal cult. These specialized groups are often referred to by the Greek term *phyle* ('brotherhood'), which connotes both their restricted membership and their adoption of corporate male identities, loosely modelled on the organization of ships' crews. As with most such experiments in social engineering, the institutional ideal of the pyramid town was quickly undermined by the complexities of social life. Within a few generations, new neighbourhoods sprang up along their intended perimeter walls. This twofold pattern of urban growth—centrally planned spaces giving way to less formally organized, but more durable communities—repeated itself throughout the history of dynastic Egypt.

Making the Body Politic

Like his Mesopotamian counterparts, the Egyptian king was entrusted with the task of securing a flow of life and blessings between heaven and earth. He did this, not by building houses for the gods, but by shaping his own body into a sacred vessel from which food offerings flowed upwards towards them, but also back down towards the dead in their tombs. Both types of feeding, the feeding of the gods and of the dead, were achieved through the ritual medium of cult statues, installed within temples and tombs.

Depictions in the tombs of Old Kingdom officials demonstrate the special relationship that existed in Egypt between cult statues and the ritually transfigured bodies of the elite dead, a relationship which finds no ready parallel in Mesopotamia. In these carved and painted scenes, the movement of the statue by sledge and boat across the Nile is closely modelled on the ritual procession of the corpse towards the tomb. In reciprocal fashion, the dead body was subject to various treatments that rendered it statue-like. Before interment it was purged of polluting substances (viscera and bodily fluids), restored through an infusion of spices and aromatic oils (juniper and cedar), and then desiccated in a bath of natron ('divine salt'). Its orifices sealed with wax, the washed corpse was then wrapped in strips of linen, smeared with gum or plaster so that they stuck to the skin. Finally the body, now coated from head to toe, was carefully modelled and painted with features that evoked the appearance of the deceased in life, and also that of his cult statues, installed nearby within the offering chamber of the tomb. The equivalence of statue and body was confirmed by the performance of an Opening of the Mouth ritual upon the anthropomorphic coffin that contained the mummified corpse, during which its painted lips were touched with a sculptor's tool.

The statue's journey to the tomb was accompanied by the burning of incense, carried by an attendant in a small cup. Purification was necessary because the foods offered to the cult statue were not ordinary goods. As confirmed by the standard offering formula inscribed within the tomb chapel (which begins: 'An offering which the king gives to Osiris') they were the residues of sacrifices performed by the king for the gods, who had already partaken of their share. Their ingestion by the dead was therefore an act of communion, which required the establishment of a pure environment around the statue. The offering formula was inscribed next to an image of the deceased seated at a table heaped with bread, portions of meat, and other offerings, enumerated by the thousand (the 'small change' of divine favour). Inscriptions accompanying the offering scene list special roles possessed by the tomb-owner during life, ordered by rank. Among the most prestigious we find titles relating to the personal regime of the king—in particular, the ritual management of substances emitted by the royal body (hair, nails) and of artefacts in contact with its skin (wigs, cosmetics, jewellery, clothing).

As Wolfgang Helck (1954) noted long ago, elite funerary biographies affirm the unique status of the king's body as an earthly container and conduit of sacred power. This status is already clearly apparent on the earliest royal monuments, dating to the end of the fourth millennium BC. All are ceremonial editions of portable instruments, used since Neolithic times for the ritual care and protection of the body: stone palettes for the grinding of pigments and medicines, combs for grooming and fastening the hair, and also weapons such as knives and maces. Together they form a ritual kit for the manipulation of fluids that entered and left the body by rubbing, ingestion, or the opening of the skin. These actions of containment and release are dramatized in their surface imagery. Carved in high relief (a technique later reserved for temple walls) they depict in miniature a world of chaotic forces located on the margins of the Nile alluvium. The king appears in this world as a dominant force, taking the guise of lethally dangerous animals that guard its frontiers.

In later periods, the representation of the royal body as co-extensive with the margins of the cosmos was carried over and extended on the monumental walls of temples serving the royal funerary cult. Valley temples, located close to the floodplain, were attached to royal pyramid tombs by monumental stone causeways. The mummified body and cult statues of the king travelled along these ceremonial routes on their respective journeys to the burial chamber, and to the mortuary chapel where the offering cult was established. The decorative programme of the funerary temples and causeway translated this movement into a grandiose statement of the king's magnetic force, which gathers the resources of the royal domain towards his body, prior to its entry to the tomb. Gifts of agricultural produce arrive from estates across the country, which are represented as subordinate 'bodies' of land, their personified forms marching along the walls of the temple, offerings in hand. The procession of the royal body to the tomb also causes materials to arrive from spaces beyond the alluvium. Non-Egyptians appear in these scenes as carriers of tribute, or as human tribute in the form of slaves, compelled towards the royal figure. We see the arrival of incense from *Punt* together with myrrh seedlings, which the king cultivates in Egyptian soil, a theme represented in the Old Kingdom temple of Sahure at Abusir, and repeated centuries later in the New Kingdom temple of Queen Hatshupsut, at Deir el-Bahri. Precious oils and exotic animals are brought to him in homage on sailing ships from Byblos; and human captives approach from Nubia and Libya, bound and led by the gods of Egypt.

In celebrating the king's superhuman capacity to draw in and consume precious resources, the external decorative programme of the funerary complex forms our clearest thematic counterpart to the temple-building activities of Mesopotamian kings. These scenes, and the activities they framed, formed a prelude to more restricted rituals that accompanied the movement of the royal body into the pyramid tomb. There the person of the king entered a new phase of transformation, intended to grant him the full characteristics of a god, and to secure his successful departure from the mortal world. Magical incantations (known as 'Pyramid Texts'), inscribed on the walls of royal burial chambers during the later part of the Old Kingdom, preserve commentaries that accompanied the ritual preparation of the body for its onward journey. The rituals themselves, which were most likely carried out elsewhere, culminated in the body's consecration and ritual 'opening' for the receipt of offerings. Reference is made to the burning of incense, described as the 'sweat' and 'odour of the gods', which drives out the offensive stench of the rotting corpse. The fragrant smoke also forms a channel of communication between heaven and earth. Under tangled cover of its rising folds, the king is able to transcend the distance between the divine and human spheres:

> The fire is laid, the fire shines;
> The incense is laid on the fire, the incense shines.
> Your perfume comes to me, O Incense;
> May my perfume come to you, O Incense.
> Your perfume comes to me, you gods;
> May my perfume come to you, you gods.
> May I be with you, you gods;
> May you be with me, you gods.

And shortly after:

> ...Here comes the climber, here comes the climber!
> Here comes he who flew up, here comes he who flew up!
> I ascend upon the thighs of Isis,
> I climb upon the thighs of Nephtys,
> My father Atum seizes my hand for me,
> And he assigns me to those excellent and wise gods,
> The Imperishable Stars.

> (After Nielsen 1986)

Another series of utterances, inscribed within the pyramid of Unas, characterizes the transfiguration of the

king in a different way. In order to join the company of
the gods, he must first overcome his dependence on their
offerings, and regain control of his own food supply. He
does this by an act of cannibalism, literally eating his way
out of the earthly realm and back to a condition of whole-
ness that evokes the primeval unity of the cosmos. What
the king devours along the way are the bodies of the gods
themselves, and the magical substances they contain:

> They have seen Unas, risen, empowered,
> As a god living on his fathers, feeding on his mothers.
> . . . .
>
> It is Unas who is the Lord of Offerings, who ties the rope,
> And provides his own offering meal himself.
> Unas it is who eats people, who lives on gods.
> . . . .
>
> It is Unas who eats their magic, who swallows their souls.
> . . . .
>
> He is replete. Their magic is in his belly.
> . . . .
>
> Unas has swallowed the perception of every god.
> Eternity is the lifespan of Unas; the end of time is his end.
>
> (Excerpt from 'The Cannibal Hymn'; after Eyre 2002)

The king does not consume the other gods directly, but
in a series of stages, and via the intermediary figure of a
sacrificial animal. The object of sacrifice, called Bull of
the Sky, appears early on in the ritual sequence, and is
initially anything but a victim. Identified with the king,
he roams among the gods as a victorious conqueror,
feeding on their magic and taking it into his own belly.
It is the king himself who then lassoes, hobbles, and

weakens the bull. There follows a series of spells that euphorize the activities of killing, butchery, and consumption. Gods swiftly arrive on the scene to assist in decapitating the bull, removing its innards, and building a hearth on which its dismembered parts are cooked in cauldrons.

Here—just as in the culmination of Gudea's temple hymn—we find an inversion of the canonical procedures by which kings prepared food for the gods. The lighting of braziers and the roasting of offerings, whose rising fumes express the distance between heaven and earth, is notable now by its absence. Instead the sacrificial meat of the bull is boiled in a closed cauldron, which seals and contains its juices, marking the king's return to the family of the gods, whose female members emerge to stir the stew in the pot. His ascendance to a state of divinity is finally affirmed by a denial of exchange in the treatment of the sacrificial meal. The king consumes the bull in its entirety, leaving nothing aside; not even the bones or poisonous gall bladder, so that there is nothing to be shared out. With this last act of self-fashioning, he leaves behind him the society of mortals—the world of exchanges, mixtures, and borrowings—and ascends to the enduring stars.

PART II

FORGETTING THE OLD REGIME

9

ENLIGHTENMENT FROM
A DARK SOURCE

Who built Thebes of the seven gates?
In the books you will read the names of kings.
Did the kings haul up the lumps of rock?
And Babylon, many times demolished,
Who raised it up so many times?
… So many reports.
So many questions.

Bertolt Brecht, *Questions from
a Worker who Reads* (1947)

Antiquity and modernity are cut from the same cloth. That is to say, our sense of things being 'ancient' is produced—both historically and in practice—by the sense that we ourselves are 'modern'. Of course artefacts and other archaeological remains have an objective age, which can be measured in absolute terms, for instance by the rate at which radioactive isotopes decay in organic matter. But when we declare a particular institution, form of behaviour, artistic style, or belief system to be 'ancient' we are engaged in a measuring process of a quite different kind. It is our own distinctiveness, our difference from the past, that is being asserted.

In previous chapters I have been concerned in various ways with the experience of distance in past societies: the distance between the sources of raw materials and their points of consumption, and the related distance between mortals and the gods with whom they seek communion. In this and the chapter that follows, my attention shifts to the perceived distance between antiquity and modernity, and more specifically between 'ancient East' and 'modern West'. This does not signal a departure from concrete realities into the realms of theoretical abstraction. Rather I am concerned here with the curious double-life of ancient Near Eastern artefacts and images, as keys to the remote past and symbols of a changing present. In particular I want to suggest that our paradoxical understanding of the Near East—as both the birthplace of civilization and its cultural antithesis—is not just a distant legacy, tacitly passed down to us from ancient Greek and Roman sources. It is also a distinct product of modern Europe's attempt to grapple with its own, more recent history of sacral kings and dynastic power.

European Antiquity and the Problem of Kingship

It is a common misconception that the professional discipline we now call archaeology has its roots in the romantic pursuits of amateur collectors and enthusiasts.

The very term 'antiquarian' has become synonymous with this stereotypical figure of the imagination: a hobbyist whose engagement with the relics of a remote past is little more than an aimless search for oddities and aesthetic curios. We might spare a condescending smile for the hopelessly inaccurate attempts by former generations—working without the benefit of radio-carbon dating—to construct a chronology for the early phases of human development, or cast an admiring backward glance at those whose speculations appear to anticipate our current state of knowledge. Only rarely, however, do we reflect upon the political activism that motivated Europe's early antiquaries—their close involvement in the constitutional crises of their day; and the intimate relationship between revolutionary polit-ical movements and the growth of the 'archaeological imagination'.

When sixteenth-century antiquarians like Henry Spelman and François Hotman delved into the pre-Roman past of Britain and France it was, as John Pocock (1957) has demonstrated, with political subversion in mind. Most were practicing lawyers, well aware that their reconstructions of prehistory—still largely based upon Roman sources—had direct implications in the field of constitutional law. The freedoms enshrined in the French 'assembly of the nation', the English 'parliament', and the Scandinavian *riksrad* all gained legal currency from their purported origins in a remote past. All were defended in terms of their customary status, as the prod-ucts of a long evolutionary process extending back to a time before kings and written records. For (so went the logic) what kings had not created, they could not hope to suppress. 'We may never know', writes Pocock (1957: 191), 'how much of our sense of history is due to the presence in Europe of systems of customary law, and to the ideal-ization of the concept of custom which took place towards the end of the sixteenth century.'

The movement was a relatively brief one, superseded in the seventeenth century by John Locke's defence of political liberty as a preordained condition of Nature. But from the Danube to the Atlantic seaboard it ignited a new sense that history could be discovered, not just in royal annals, but in the slow development of customary practices. The unnumbered dead of antiquity were recognized as carriers of cultural wisdom and national identity, and an interest in recording their material remains—the enigmatic megaliths and tumuli that dotted the landscapes of northern Europe—became increasingly common, among both conservative and republican thinkers.

If the study of European prehistory can be consid-ered, to that extent, a legacy of republican idealism, then what we might ask were the social and ideological forces that fostered the scientific study of the ancient Near East: the proverbial birthplace of sacred kingship? How have those forces shaped and limited our perception of ancient Egypt and Mesopotamia, and their place in world history? And, to echo Brecht's enlightened artisan, we might also ask what alternative histories and connec-tions do they mask?

The Taint of Babel: Isaac Newton and the Ancient Near East

The Original of Monarchies, written in the aftermath of the 'Glorious Revolution' of 1688, is among the least well-known works of Sir Isaac Newton. For reasons unclear the essay was never completed, although fragments appear in his *Chronology of Ancient Kingdoms Amended* (1728). Much of the surviving text is devoted to constructing a reliable chronology for the earliest periods of human history, bringing the newly discovered laws of mathematics and astronomy to bear upon the writings of the Old Testament, Homer, and the Greco-Roman historians. Sifting and comparing the ancient sources in search of suggestive anomalies, Newton deposes the familiar heroes and deities of the ancient world from their local dominions over heaven and earth, forcing them to inhabit a shared universe, and to obey its rules of motion and change. Solomon and David tread the same earth as Priam and Hector. Cadmos, Europa, and the Argonauts follow the same stars as the Egyptian inventors of navigation described in Manetho's *Aegyptiaca*. The same planets orbit the walls of Troy, the temples of Byblos and Paphos, and the pyramids of Memphis.

Newton's writings on early kingship also contain the germ of a hypothesis that later generations of scholars were to advance with much greater force: that the 'arts of urban life' were not discovered in Europe, but had been brought there from the earlier civilizations of

Egypt and Mesopotamia, the lands on the Nile and the Euphrates. In Newton's day this process of transmission was linked to the dispersal of humanity at the Tower of Babel, an 'event' then placed at 2400 BC, roughly midway between the creation of the world and the time of Christ. But Newton's ancient Near East was not merely a font of technological innovations. It was also a source of cultural contamination, still carrying with it the moral taint of Babel. The scientific revolution of his own day may have had its remote beginnings in the technological achievements of the ancient Near East, but those achievements had been siphoned into a morbid and backward culture of mausoleums and wasteful luxury, ancestral to the absolute monarchies whose power in his native England had only recently been curbed. The earliest glimmers of Enlightenment had come from a dark source that produced—not only farming, literacy, astronomy, and navigation—but also sacred kingship and the dynastic cult of the dead. Only when exposed to the 'new light' of European learning could they be liberated, retrospectively, from that dark moon of superstition and intolerance, and redeemed as part of a new story of human progress, culminating in the rule of Reason and Law.

By the end of the nineteenth century this ambivalent approach to the ancient Near East had become integral to the new academic disciplines which resulted from the decipherment of the hieroglyphic and cuneiform scripts. The very names which they were given—Egyptology and Assyriology—distinguished these fields from the study of ancient Greece and Rome, reflecting their ambiguous status between the humanistic search for 'self' and the scientific study of the 'other'. The tension is clearly evident in the pioneering works of scholars such as Breasted (e.g. *The Dawn of Conscience*, 1934) and V. Gordon Childe, whose popular syntheses of European and Near Eastern archaeology—among them *New Light on the Most Ancient East* (1934) and *Man Makes Himself* (1936)—set an intellectual agenda that remains influential today. Flowing through these, and many other foundational works on ancient Egypt and Mesopotamia, we find a remarkably unified (yet in many ways paradoxical) vision of the journey taken by 'civilization' in what was by then perceived as its inexorable movement from ancient East to modern West.

A Miraculous Conception? 'Civilization' between East and West

What, then, did this meta-history of the human career consist of? A point of entry is provided by the tympanum which ornaments the entrance to the Oriental Institute in Chicago, founded in 1919 as a 'laboratory for the study of the development of civilization'. Designed under the guidance of the Institute's founder, James Henry Breasted, its relief decoration depicts the encounter between East and West. In the centre of the scene an ancient Egyptian scribe hands a fragment of a hieroglyphic inscription to a figural representation of the West. Each is flanked by a series of icons—some human, others architectural—which make clear their symbolic roles as representatives of two distinct cultural lineages. The personification of the West, in his role as recipient of the gift of writing, stands before three buildings: the Athenian Acropolis, a Gothic cathedral, and a modern skyscraper. He is in the company of Herodotus, Alexander the Great, Julius Caesar, and a series of anonymous figures who personify more recent links between the histories of East and West: a crusader, an archaeologist, and a historian of art. The symbolic landscape inhabited by the Egyptian figure comprises the palace of Persepolis in western Iran (once the seat of Achaemenid kingship), the Sphinx, and the Pyramids of Giza. He stands at the head of a group of great kings, including Hammurabi the lawgiver, each drawn from a different segment of the ancient Near East, from Persia to Egypt.

Through a further, more subtle, device—the foregrounding of the lion and buffalo as representative totems of East and West—the design places the distinction between these two lineages in the realm of nature rather than culture. East and West are presented as 'species' of a different kind, and their intercourse is made possible only under the supernatural and purifying glow of a divine sun-disc, copied from the temple reliefs of the Egyptian ruler Akhenaton, whose religious reforms are often equated with the origins of monotheism. The overall design is symmetrical, and hence the meeting of East and West appears to be one of equals. Yet the protagonists are not contemporaries. They occupy different spaces of time. Ancient Near East meets modern West, and civilization passes between them in a direct exchange that excludes altogether the more recent history of the Middle East. Modern civilization, in this scheme of representation, is a unique possession of the West, but one nevertheless built upon (ancient) Eastern foundations.

Back to the Future

On 15 April 2003, the distinguished American general Jay Montgomery Garner stood within sight of the ancient ziggurat of Ur in southern Iraq, forty centuries of history looking down upon him, and hailed the beginnings of 'a free Iraq' in 'the birthplace of civilization'. For a brief moment the miraculous image depicted on the Chicago tympanum—civilization reborn through the harmonious intercourse of ancient East and modern West—took centre stage in the present. But the sentiment (not to mention the stage management) belonged more to the Napoleonic era than to our own. And as Edward Said (1978) has argued, it is above all to that era that we should look in order to grasp the origins of attitudes that 'still dominate our contemporary cultural and political perspectives' on the ancient Near (and modern, Middle) East.

In doing so, however, we should be wary of reducing European engagements with the ancient Near Eastern past to an exercise in cultural domination, and of reproducing timeless oppositions between the viewpoints of 'East' and 'West'. Bonaparte's 'liberation' of Egypt, to which the following chapter turns, was accompanied by a carefully coordinated scientific mission, laying institutional foundations for a systematic investigation and recovery of Egypt's ancient past. Despite its military failures, the Napoleonic expedition provided a model, soon followed by other European powers, for extending the study of Western origins directly, and more widely, into the ancestral lands of the Near East, setting in motion the establishment of research centres, museums, and fieldwork schools—from Athens to Baghdad—that exist to this day.

Recent military action in Iraq by America and Britain has, in only partial contrast, been accompanied by the looting of museums and the destruction of archaeological sites on an industrial scale: a tragedy often reported in the popular press—and with little sense of historical irony—as a savage attack by the Iraqi people upon the unguarded 'cradle of civilization'. We might also recall that the Napoleonic encounter with the Near East unfolded at a crucial turning point in European history. For many ordinary 'occidentals' the French Revolution of 1789, following swiftly on the heels of the American War of Independence, meant more than the overthrow of the Bourbon monarchy. It also promised the closure of a long chapter in human history: the end of the 'dynastic realm', for centuries the only imaginable system of government in much of Europe, and the dawn of a new political age.

10

RUINED REGIMES: EGYPT AT THE REVOLUTION

Hail solitary ruins, holy sepulchres and silent walls!
When the whole earth, in chains and silence, bowed
the neck before its tyrants, you had already
proclaimed the truths which they abhor; and,
confounding the dust of the king with that of the
meanest slave, had announced to man the sacred
dogma of Equality.

> Comte de Volney, *Les ruines, ou Méditation sur les
> revolutions des empires* (1791)

That dead man is Old France, and that bier, the
coffin of the Old Monarchy.

> Jules Michelet, *Histoire de la Révolution
> française* (1879–80)

I n her *Festivals and the French Revolution* (1988), Mona
Ozouf evokes the republican 'theatre state' that
commandeered the streets of Paris in the aftermath of
the revolutionary Terror, which saw the brutal deposition of France's *ancien régime*. Simulacra of royal and

163

religious relics—statues, images, sceptres—were burned and broken, and at Morteau the 'Burial of Monarchy' was enacted, as if to speed it forcibly into an antiquarian domain of ruin and loss: 'for although the legislator makes the laws for the people, festivals make the people for the laws'. Prominent within these remarkable performances was a range of imagery inspired by ancient Egypt.

In 1792 the Conseil Géneral de la Commune ordered that a prominent statue of Louis XVI in the Place des Victoires be demolished and replaced by an obelisk (wrongly described in their directive as a 'pyramid') inscribed with the names of fallen revolutionary leaders. The same year witnessed a major festival in the Tuileries for the martyrs of the Revolution, at which the focal monument was an enormous wooden pyramid. A leaflet was distributed requiring each citizen to place a garland at its base in honor of those heroes 'who helped us to vanquish the tyrants!' One year later, a monumental statue of the goddess of Nature, bedecked in ancient Egyptian costume, was erected on the ruins of the Bastille for the Festival of Regeneration. Water spouted from her breasts into a basin below, where speeches were made celebrating the return of the people to an original state of innocence and freedom.

The ideological background to this choice of imagery is found in the (1791) meditations of the Comte de Volney, a leading republican, on the ruins of the Orient. Published during the early stages of revolution in France, and swiftly translated into English, they relate the experiences of a traveller passing through the lands of the Near East, then still under the control of the Ottoman Empire. Resting among the remains of an ancient city on the Syrian steppe, he is confronted by a ghostly apparition who reveals to him a terrifying vision: the banks of the Seine and the Thames have become a landscape of monumental ruins, like those of the Nile and the Euphrates through which he passes. Civilization and progress have passed by the gaudy palaces of Old Europe, moving along on their westward march to the newly liberated shores of the New World, where freedom flourishes unfettered by the burdens of history and monarchy. In a penetrating analysis of *Les ruines*, Peter Hughes (1995) detects a need to commemorate the pre-Revolutionary world of the Bourbon court, even as it was being condemned to oblivion. Ruins, he observes, offer 'a way of overcoming the absence of the past when it is limited to paper and ink or condemned to fading memory'. Remembering Egypt, in Jan Assmann's (1997: 7–8) words, then becomes a 'liberation from one's own past which is no longer one's own ... Egypt must be remembered in order to know what lies in the past, and what must not be allowed to come back.'

Revolutionary thought, in all times and places, requires a sense both of the naturalness of its own aims and of the unnaturalness of what it seeks to overthrow. The experience of the French Revolution, and the chronic social instability and periodic relapses into old forms of authority that followed, raised urgent new questions. How does a society function without rulers? What is the place and responsibility of the individual within the collective? Is secular knowledge adequate to replace the precepts of a hierocratic order? New ideas were needed to make the vision of a modern future understandable as part of a natural evolution from the past: ideas about the forces of cohesion and change that bind human beings together into stable 'societies', and which in time induce some of those societies to move through different 'phases of civilization', while others (as Samuel Huntington put it, more recently) 'disappear and are buried in the sands of time'. Time itself, as Ozouf observes, 'was not merely the formal framework within which the Revolution took place; it was also the raw material on which it obstinately worked'. And as a central requirement of the work of modernity the institution of kingship—together with all its antique trappings—had to be pushed to the margins of historical consciousness and rendered anomalous, exotic, and moribund: frozen in time.

'Liberating' Egypt and Forgetting the *Ancien Régime*

These were among the social and ideological forces at play when Britain's growing hold on Mughal India and the eastern trade prompted Napoleon Bonaparte to invade Egypt in 1798. With the embers of the French Revolution still burning on the streets of Paris, the chief servant of the Directory confronted the Ottoman Empire in the name of liberty, and in the process encountered the ancient kings of the Nile Valley. Faced with this spectacle, the general of the First Republic could not resist entombing himself briefly within the Great Pyramid. But the irony was short-lived. It was not to a pharaonic legacy that Napoleon appealed in his victorious address to the people of Alexandria, but to an idealized Islamic past of flourishing cities and trade, free from the yoke of Mameluke tyranny. And it was with his domestic subjects, rather than the people of Egypt, in mind that the 167 savants who accompanied the expedition were set to the task of documenting and appropriating the ancient monuments.

The publication of the monumental *Description de l'Égypte* (1809–28) was commemorated by the striking of a bronze medallion designed by J. J. Barre. It shows a masculine personification of Roman Gaul unveiling ancient Egypt in the form of a suppliant woman, who fondles the muzzle of a crocodile upon which she reclines. She holds a sistrum to evoke the goddess Hathor, and hence female sexuality, whose temple at Dendera is faithfully depicted in the background. She is, in short, a carefully crafted antithesis to 'Marianne': the female embodiment of republican virtue and reason, whose vigorous form—a forerunner to the Statue of Liberty—came to symbolize the victory of 'the people' in the official iconography of the Revolution. Undoubtedly concerned with discovery and appropriation, the image is also a powerful allegory for the pacifying and feminizing of an alien power, represented by the pyramids which are visible behind the figure of Gaul. The motif of 'unveiling Egypt' further represents the end of

Egypt's special status as a source of esoteric wisdom, used since medieval times to bolster the authority of European dynasts.

The reality of the French advance through Egypt was, naturally, a more prosaic and brutal one. We are fortunate in having a first-hand account—the diary of Capt. Joseph-Marie Moiret—to set against the official representations that emerged in later decades. At the Battle of the Pyramids, Moiret's forces helped to overcome a Mameluke cavalry armed with sabres and guns supplied by the British government. 'We burned to surpass the pagan heroes', he wrote, 'and to avenge the spilled blood of our Christian forefathers.' In the event victory was decided, not by the heroic charge of the Gallic warrior—as later depicted on the frontispiece of the *Description*—but by the cold discipline of massed infantry. 'No battle', remarked General Berthier, 'has ever shown more clearly the superiority of European tactics over the undisciplined courage of the Orient.'

On a torch-lit September night, as the floodwaters of the Nile began their annual retreat, residents of Cairo were confronted with an unusual spectacle. French soldiers had gathered around a 'pyramid', specially constructed in the centre of Ezbekieh Square, and inscribed with the names of comrades fallen in the struggle against 'Mameluke tyranny'. Encircling the monument were banners proclaiming 'Hail the French Republic', but also 'God is God, and Muhammad his Prophet'. Soldiers had been instructed to win the hearts and minds of the Egyptian people, as well as their ports and cities. On that night they were celebrating the Festival of the Republic, which culminated in a public declaration—authored by Bonaparte—that the 'era of democratic government' was now upon Egypt, land of immemorial kingship. Yet democracy, it transpired, was far from secure in France itself, and the finer points of the speech were anyway lost on Moiret's hungry and battle-worn troops, whose devotion 'had always been to the father-land, not to this or that form of government'.

Almost a century later the acclaimed military artist Maurice Orange produced an image which captures the paradox of the Napoleonic encounter with Egypt. By 1895, the date of its composition, France had endured some four convulsive shifts between dynastic and republican forms of government. Orange's Napoleon stands before the Great Pyramid: the chief servant of the Directory confronting the mummified body of an ancient Egyptian king, newly excavated from the ground. Its wrappings have begun to fall away, or have perhaps been deliberately removed, exposing a face unaffected by the passing of centuries. The painting may be taken to evoke timeless themes such as the transience of power; equally it could be read as a satirical commentary on Napoleon's own imperial ambitions. Yet it also poses a distinctly modern dilemma, to which Orange's generation was more alive than our own: how to commit the memory of kingship, once and for all, to the ground? How, as Jules Michelet put it in his impassioned history of the French Revolution, to 'bury, and for ever, the dreams in which we once fondly trusted—paternal royalty, the government

169

of grace, the clemency of the monarchy, and the charity of the priest; filial confidence, implicit belief in the gods here below'. For the dead king of Orange's painting does not belong fully to the past. His whiskered face is unmistakably that of Louis-Napoléon, last ruler of France before the establishment of the Third Republic, and a historical counterpart—in that sense—to the unfortunate Kaiser Wilhelm, whose own strange relationship with the ancient Near East I have already touched on. Bonaparte's true encounter is not, then, with a remote civilization, but with what Michelet called the 'vampires' of Europe's own old regime, rising from the dead to lay claim to a future as yet unborn.

The Cruel Museum and the Laughing People

In 1793 the opening of the Palais du Louvre as a public institution, the Museum Central des Arts, signalled the democratization of 'high culture' in France. The former royal residence became a venue for the display of an extraordinary quantity of art objects confiscated by Bonaparte's forces following their successful campaigns in Belgium (1794) and Italy (1796–9) and was renamed the Musée Napoleon in 1803. In a letter to Bonaparte the Commissioner of Art, André Thouin, expressed his view that 'the French spoliation of Italy was the reward of military virtue over decadence and that this was strictly comparable with what the Greeks are supposed to have done to the Egyptians and the Romans in their turn to the Greeks'. As Cecil Gould (1965: 13, 40) put it,

Europe's first state museum 'was born of three parents, republicanism, anti-clericalism, and successful aggressive war ... The Revolution had set up an idol which itself demanded the offerings that were made to it.'

Only in 1826, under the briefly restored monarchy of Charles X, was a section devoted to ancient Egypt. Its curator, Jean François Champollion, had recently announced his successful decipherment of the hieroglyphic script, heralding the foundation of Egyptology as a modern discipline. Two galleries were set aside for royal funerary practices, one for precious items and materials, and a fourth for religious beliefs. The ceiling of the latter chamber was adorned with an allegorical painting portraying a transition from the decadence of tyranny to the rewards of enlightened government as *L'Étude et le Génie des arts dévoilant l'Égypte à la Gréce*. At the heart of the lavish *salle funéraire* stood a large platform on which were arranged the upper casings of elaborate sarcophagi, their lower casings—containing the miraculously preserved bodies of the Egyptian elite— placed unceremoniously on the floor beneath.

Here any citizen could stand alongside royalty and measure their own being against the exposed figure of a divine king, while at the same time measuring the human size of the latter against that of his boastful monuments, a selection of which was also exhibited. On display to the people of Paris was not merely the fantastic 'otherness' of Oriental civilization, but also the very embodiment of dynastic rule, displaced onto the inscrutable remains of an ancient culture and located safely

171

behind the threshold of modernity. The guillotine had given way to the intrusive public gaze as a means of unveiling and laying to rest the ghost of monarchy. In this sense the museum anticipated, in concrete form, the grand themes of Michelet's (1879–80) *Histoire de la Révolution française*, and a new apprehension of the human past:

Another thing which this History will clearly establish and holds true in every respect is that the people were usually more important than the leaders. The deeper I have excavated, the more surely I have satisfied myself that the best was underneath, in the obscure depths... To find the people again and put it back in its proper role, I have been obliged to reduce to their proportions the ambitious marionettes whose strings it manipulated and in whom hitherto we have looked for and thought to see the secret play of history.

Looking back upon the Napoleonic era from our own perspective, we can recognize—more clearly than we otherwise might—the formation of those cultural lenses through which we now habitually view the remains of the ancient Near East. We have become accustomed to the cruelty of the modern state museum and its carnival-like parodies of sacred kingship. We have come to expect and even relish the sight of monumental gates leading nowhere, proud royal statues flanking nothing, once-hidden gods now revealed in transparent cases, and carefully preserved corpses exposed for inspection: the eviscerated 'body politic' rendered impotent, bizarre, even comical. And so we return to the theme of distance, and to the emotional distance between subjects and sacred kings which—with the fall of Old Regimes, from Boston Harbour and Paris to Shahyad Square in Tehran—has been gradually remoulded into new relationships between 'society' and various forms of 'the state'. Antiquity and modernity, cut from the same cloth.

CONCLUSION:
WHAT MAKES CIVILIZATION?

Our conventional image of the ancient Near East as the 'cradle of Western civilization' can no longer be taken for granted. Why, some scholars are asking, should the early achievements of Mesopotamia and Egypt be viewed as a mere prelude to 'the rise of the West', when there are other stories to be told, and other links between past and present to be explored? Yet in a different—and contradictory—vein, historians of the classical world have recently been chastised for failing to adequately acknowledge the cultural debt owed by Greece to the ancient Near East.

Behind these scholarly debates lie hard political and economic realities. For many modern states in the Middle East, the pre-Islamic past represents a gateway for Western tourism; for secular forms of knowledge and identity; and for the world market. The ownership, protection, and representation of pre-Islamic cultures is now an intense focus of ideological struggle, affecting the everyday lives of communities throughout the region.

As the remains of the past are drawn with increasing ferocity into the conflicts of the present, it is worth reflecting on the lessons we stand to learn from the ancient Near East. What conclusions can we draw from the myriad collections of artefacts and site reports accumulated over a century of research?

If the parallel development of Mesopotamia and Egypt demonstrates anything, it is surely the deep attachment of human societies to the concepts they live by, and the inequalities they are prepared to endure in order to preserve those guiding principles. Certain basic notions of how the world should be made and ordered—by keeping the house beautiful or the body pure—remained constant (and constantly distinct) in these two regions for thousands of years, despite the interactions between them, and despite changes in almost every other field of life. The desire to realize this sense of order, and the sacrifices demanded in the process, produced astonishing flows of materials, transforming societies and reshaping environments from Afghanistan to Turkey, and from the forests of Lebanon to the deserts of Arabia.

But the gods were never satisfied. Their work was never done. In contemplating yet another remaking of our own world order, there is surely something here for us to learn. Civilizations, from the perspective of history, are shown to be the outcome of mixtures and borrowings, often of quite arbitrary things, but always on a prodigious scale. Their study draws us into a grand narrative of the past, a story built from the ground up by routine human activities, surpassing the limited purview of any one society, and of such a magnitude as to worry the gods. Yet by elevating civilizations to the pinnacle of human achievement, or seeking to orientate our future around an idealized image of what they might become, are we not simply raising up new gods where old ones have fallen? The problem, it seems, is both as old as time and as fresh as our tomorrows.

FURTHER READING

To systematically compare the early development of Egyptian and Mesopotamian society, as Henri Frankfort so ably managed more than half a century ago in his *The Birth of Civilization in the Near East* (1951), would today require a study many times this length. Existing volumes, mostly dedicated to one or other region, provide systematic treatments of social institutions, architecture, settlement patterns, religion and ritual, artistic styles, and scripts, at a much finer resolution than has been possible here. Nor have I attempted to add to the many existing accounts of 'great excavations', or to assess the intellectual development of disciplines such as archaeology, Egyptology, and Assyriology: topics already covered by an extensive literature, some of which is referenced below. In such a short book, I have focused instead upon a number of core problems and questions, as laid out in the Preface and Introduction.

What follows is a chapter-by-chapter commentary, giving the main sources upon which I have drawn. For purposes of brevity and accessibility I have concentrated upon the more readily available literature, and upon English-language texts, particularly those offering stepping stones to the more specialized studies contained in scholarly journals. The latter are omitted here except where they have a direct bearing upon points of argument in the chapters. At the end of each section I also supply a list of works referred to directly and, where appropriate, links to accredited websites carrying the results of current field excavations and other useful resources.

For readers seeking more general overviews of ancient Egypt and Mesopotamia, a number can be mentioned at the outset. For Mesopotamia, the best general introduction is Nicholas Postgate's *Early Mesopotamia: Society and Economy at the Dawn of History* (New York: Routledge, 1996), while more detailed discussion of the periods covered in this book is provided by Susan Pollock in her *Ancient Mesopotamia: The Eden That Never Was* (Cambridge: Cambridge University Press, 1999). Barry Kemp's *Ancient Egypt: Anatomy of a Civilization*, 2nd edn (London: Routledge, 2006) provides a stimulating and richly documented interpretation of dynastic society down to the end of the New Kingdom; David Wengrow's *The Archaeology of Early Egypt: Social Transformations in North-East Africa, 10,000 to 2650 BC* (Cambridge: Cambridge University Press, 2006) covers the prehistoric period and early dynasties with extensive references, and provides further background to some of the ideas explored in this book. Outstanding surveys of each region, with colour illustrations, are John Baines and Jaromír Málek's *Cultural Atlas of Ancient Egypt*, rev. edn (New York: Facts on File, 2000) and Michael Roaf's *Cultural Atlas of Mesopotamia and the Ancient Near East* (New York: Facts on File, 2000).

Many aspects of Egyptian and Mesopotamian culture and society are expertly reviewed, with further references, in Jack M. Sasson et al. (eds.), *Civilizations of the Ancient Near East* (New York: Charles Scribner's Sons, 1995). This four-volume collection also contains informative essays on the historical reception and study of the ancient Near East in Europe, from antiquity to the twentieth century AD. Amélie Kuhrt's *The Ancient Near East, c.3000–330 BC*, 2 vols (New York/London: Routledge, 1995) is the best general synthesis of historical sources from the earliest writing to the time of Alexander the Great. Another excellent survey, but more narrowly focused upon Mesopotamia, is Marc Van De Mieroop's *A History of the Ancient Near East, ca.3000–323 BC* (Malden, MA/Oxford: Blackwell, 2004). For art and architecture, see Henri Frankfort, *The Art and Architecture of the Ancient Orient*, 5th edn., with commentary by Michael Roaf and Donald Matthews (New Haven, CT/London: Yale University Press, 1996); and William Stevenson Smith, *The Art and Architecture of Ancient Egypt*, 3rd edn., rev. William Kelly Simpson (New Haven, CT/London: Yale University Press, 1998).

Bruce Trigger's *Understanding Early Civilizations* (Cambridge: Cambridge University Press, 2003) treats Egypt and Mesopotamia alongside Shang China, the Aztecs, and other ancient societies in the search for a general definition of 'early civilization'. It may be contrasted with an essay by John Baines and Norman Yoffee, exploring the comparison between Egypt and Mesopotamia for the light it sheds on local sequences of social and political development: 'Order, Legitimacy, and Wealth in Ancient Egypt and Mesopotamia', in Gary M. Feinman and Joyce Marcus (eds.), *Archaic States* (Santa Fe, NM: School of American Research Press, 1998). Both studies provide important perspectives on the themes addressed in this book, as well as much additional information.

Preface

Insofar as this book follows a particular methodology, it is contained in Emile Durkheim and Marcel Mauss's programmatic 'Note sur la notion de civilization', *Année sociologique* 12 (1913): 46–50. A translation, with commentary, is provided in Nathan Schlanger's *Marcel Mauss: Techniques, Technology and Civilization* (New York/ Oxford: Durkheim Press; Berghahn Books, 2006). My approach also draws upon Norbert Elias's analysis of *The Civilizing Process* (Oxford: Blackwell, 1990; German original, 1939) in late medieval Europe. The fate of the Iraq Museum in April of 2003 is the subject of Milbry Polk and Angela M. H. Schuster (eds.), *The Looting of the Iraq Museum, Baghdad: The Lost Legacy of Ancient Mesopotamia* (New York: Abrams, 2005). For the targeting of antiquities under ISIS occupation, see Eleanor Robson, 'Modern war, ancient casualties'. TLS—The Times Literary Supplement (26 March 2015), pp. 11–12.

Introduction: A Clash of Civilizations?

Edward Said's *Orientalism: Western Conceptions of the Orient*, 4th edn. (London: Penguin, 1995) remains essential background reading for the issues raised here. Equally fundamental is Martin Bernal's *Black Athena: The Afroasiatic Roots of Classical Civilization*, vol. 1: *The Fabrication of Ancient Greece 1785–1985* (London: Free Association Books, 1987), which argues that European views of the ancient Near East, and its contribution to Western culture, have been strongly distorted by racist and imperialist agendas since the eighteenth century. Bernal's own, subsequent reconstructions of cultural interrelations in the Bronze Age Mediterranean have been widely criticized on empirical grounds, as has his implicit view that Egypt's contribution to world history must be gauged in terms of its influence upon Greek civilization. For a representative range of responses, see Mary R. Lefkowitz and Guy MacLean Rogers (eds.), *Black Athena Revisited* (Chapel Hill/London: University of North Carolina Press, 1996). Thomas Scheffler provides a lucid discussion of how modern geopolitics has shaped contemporary understandings of the ancient Near East: 'Fertile Crescent, Orient, Middle East: The Changing Mental Maps of Southwest Asia', *European Review of History* 10 (2003): 253–72.

Early to mid-twentieth-century essays on civilization by Lucien Febvre, Sigmund Freud, and others are brought together in John Rundell and Stephen Mennell (eds.), *Classical Readings in Culture and Civilization* (London: Routledge, 1998); and see also Franz Steiner's 1944 essay 'On the Process of Civilization', in Jeremy Adler and Richard Fardon (eds.), *Orientpolitik, Value, and Civilization* (New York/Oxford: Berghahn, 1999). Richard Overy's *The Morbid Age: Britain between the Wars* (London:

Penguin, 2009) assesses mid-twentieth-century fears over a looming crisis in Western civilization, drawing suggestive analogies with our current zeitgeist.

Other works referred to include H. Frankfort, *The Birth of Civilization in the Near East* (Bloomington: Indiana University Press, 1951); F. Fukuyama, 'The End of History?', *The National Interest* (Summer 1989); John M. Headley, 'Geography and Empire in the Late Renaissance: Botero's Assignment, Western Universalism, and the Civilizing Process', *Renaissance Quarterly* 53 (2000): 1119–55; S. P. Huntington, 'The Clash of Civilizations?', *Foreign Affairs* 72 (1993): 22–49; *idem, The Clash of Civilizations and the Remaking of World Order* (New York: Simon and Schuster, 1996); J. M. Lundquist, 'Babylon in European Thought', in Jack M. Sasson et al. (eds.), *Civilizations of the Ancient Near East* (New York: Scribner, 1995), 67–80; G. Maspero, *The Struggle of the Nations: Egypt, Syria, and Assyria* (London: Society for Promoting Christian Knowledge, 1896); C. Quigley, *The Evolution of Civilizations: An Introduction to Historical Analysis* (New York: Macmillan, 1961); E. Said, 'The Clash of Ignorance', *The Nation* (22 October 2001); H. V. F. Winstone, *Gertrude Bell* (London: Barzan, 2004).

Chapter 1. Camouflaged Borrowings

Translations of the 'The Report of Wenamun' and the 'Epic of Gilgamesh' can be found in anthologies of Egyptian and Mesopotamian literature, such as William Kelly Simpson (ed.), *The Literature of Ancient Egypt: An*

Anthology of Stories, Instructions, Stelae, Autobiographies, and Poetry (New Haven, CT/London: Yale University Press, 2003); and Stephanie Dalley, *Myths from Mesopotamia: Creation, The Flood, Gilgamesh, and Others* (Oxford/New York: Oxford University Press, 2000); see also Benjamin R. Foster, *The Epic of Gilgamesh* (New York/London: Norton, 2001). For the early history of Byblos, see Nina Jidejian, *Byblos through the Ages*, 2nd edn (Beirut: Dar An-Nahar, 2000); and also Claude Doumet-Serhal (ed.), *Decade: A Decade of Archaeology and History in Lebanon* (Beirut: Lebanese British Friends of the National Museum, 2004).

Egyptian and Mesopotamian attitudes towards, and classifications of, the outside world, are critically discussed in Mario Liverani, *Prestige and Interest: International Relations in the Near East ca.1600–1100 BC* (Padova: Sargon, 1990); David O'Connor and Stephen Quirke (eds.), *Mysterious Lands* (London: UCL Press, 2003); and Timothy Potts, *Mesopotamia and the East: An Archaeological and Historical Study of Foreign Relations ca.3400–2000 BC* (Oxford: Oxford University Committee for Archaeology, 1994). For the Ebla archives, and their historical implications, see Giovanni Pettinato, *Ebla: A New Look at History*, trans. C. Faith Richardson (Baltimore: Johns Hopkins University Press, 1991); but also the reservations expressed by Piotr Michalowski, 'Third Millennium Contacts: Observations on the Relationships between Mari and Ebla', *Journal of the American Oriental Society* 105 (1985): 293–302.

A global survey of the earliest known writing systems, their functions and development, can be found in A.-M. Christin (ed.), *A History of Writing: From Hieroglyph to Multimedia* (Paris: Flammarion, 2002). For more specialized, and often quite technical, discussions of the earliest scripts, see Stephen D. Houston (ed.), *The First Writing: Script Invention as History and Process* (Cambridge: Cambridge University Press, 2004). The interpretation of cuneiform texts is engagingly treated in Marc Van de Mieroop's *Cuneiform Texts and the Writing of History* (London/New York: Routledge, 1999). The invention and development of the Egyptian scripts is discussed from various perspectives in John Baines, *Visual and Written Culture in Ancient Egypt* (Oxford/New York: Oxford University Press, 2007).

Evidence of prehistoric irrigation systems in Iraq and Iran is discussed in G. K. Gillmore et al., 'Irrigation on the Tehran Plain, Iran: Tepe Pardis—The Site of a Possible Neolithic Irrigation Feature?', *Catena* 79 (2009): 285–300; and for early urbanization in northern Syria see Joan Oates et al., 'Early Mesopotamian Urbanism: A New View from the North', *Antiquity* 81 (2007): 585–600. Ancient Near Eastern systems of land use are further discussed in Robert M. Adams, *Heartland of Cities: Studies of Ancient Settlement and Land Use on the Central Floodplain of the Euphrates* (Chicago: University of Chicago Press, 1981), and Tony J. Wilkinson's *Archaeological Landscapes of the Near East* (Tucson: University of Arizona Press, 2003); and in the *Bulletin on Sumerian Agriculture* (Cambridge: Sumerian Agriculture Group,

1984–95). For agricultural practices in prehistoric and ancient Egypt, Karl W. Butzer's *Early Hydraulic Civilization in Egypt: A Study in Cultural Ecology* (Chicago: University of Chicago Press, 1976) remains important; and see also Alan K. Bowman and Eugene L. Rogan (eds.), *Agriculture in Egypt, from Pharaonic to Modern Times* (Oxford: Oxford University Press for the British Academy, 1999).

Other works referred to include B. Anderson, *Imagined Communities* (London/New York: Verso, 1991); K. Eckholm and J. Friedman, 'Capital Imperialism and Exploitation in Ancient World Systems', in M. T. Larsen (ed.), *Power and Propaganda: A Symposium on Ancient Empires* (Copenhagen: Akademisk Forlag, 1979), 41–58; Marcel Mauss, 'The Nation' (1920), in Nathan Schlanger, *Marcel Mauss: Techniques, Technology and Civilization* (New York/Oxford: Durkheim Press; Berghahn Books, 2006), 41–8; K. A. Wittfogel, *Oriental Despotism: A Comparative Study of Total Power* (New Haven, CT/ London: Yale University Press, 1957).

Chapter 2. On the Trail of Blue-Haired Gods

The Tell el-Farkha statue coverings are presented in Krzysztof M. Ciałowicz, *Ivory and Gold: Beginnings of Egyptian Art* (Poznań: Poznań Prehistoric Society, 2007); Tutankhamun's funerary mask and the bracelets of Shoshenq are illustrated in Jaromír Málek, *Egypt: 4000 Years of Art* (London: Phaidon, 2003). Many other objects referred to in this chapter, including material from Mari and Ur, appear in Joan Aruz (ed.), *Art of the First Cities* (New York: Metropolitan Museum of Art; New Haven, CT/London: Yale University Press, 2003), which also contains expert summaries of regional developments from the Indus to the Mediterranean in the third millennium BC.

Archaeological evidence for the manufacture of glass and faience is reviewed in Roger (P.R.S.) Moorey, *Ancient Mesopotamian Materials and Industries: The Archaeological Evidence* (Winona Lake, IN: Eisenbrauns, 1999) and in Paul T. Nicholson and Ian Shaw (eds.), *Ancient Egyptian Materials and Technology* (Cambridge: Cambridge University Press, 2000). These volumes provide authoritative and meticulously referenced overviews of Mesopotamian and Egyptian crafts, charting the changing uses of specific materials. For the use of lapis lazuli, glass, and faience in the Bronze Age Aegean, see Caroline M. Jackson and Emma C. Wagner (eds.), *Vitreous Materials in the Late Bronze Age Aegean* (Oxford: Oxbow, 2008).

For broad overviews of interregional trade see also Shereen Ratnagar, *Trading Encounters: From the Euphrates to the Indus in the Bronze Age* (New Delhi/ Oxford: Oxford University Press, 2004); Victor Mair (ed.), *Contact and Exchange in the Ancient World* (Honolulu: University of Hawaii Press, 2006); Andrew Bevan, *Stone Vessels and Values in the Bronze Age Mediterranean* (Cambridge: Cambridge University Press, 2007). For lapis lazuli at Ebla, see Giovanni Pettinato, *Ebla: A New*

Look at History, trans. C. Faith Richardson (Baltimore: Johns Hopkins University Press, 1991), and for comparisons between personal ornaments at Mohenjo-daro, Ur, and Troy, see Joan Aruz, *op. cit.* A detailed treatment of cultural and symbolic engagements with the mineral world in ancient Egypt is provided in Sydney Aufrère's *L'Univers minéral dans la pensée égyptienne* (Cairo: Institut français d'archéologie orientale, 1991).

Other works referred to include R. D. Griffith, 'Gods' blue hair in Homer and Eighteenth-Dynasty Egypt', *Classical Quarterly* 55 (2005): 329–34; D. T. Potts, *Mesopotamian Civilization: The Material Foundations* (London: Athlone Press, 1997); S. Sherratt, 'Archaeological Contexts', in J. M. Foley (ed.), *A Companion to Ancient Epic* (Malden, MA/Oxford: Wiley-Blackwell, 2005).

Chapter 3. Neolithic Worlds

For the deliberate deposition of lapis lazuli and other materials in temple foundations, see Richard S. Ellis, *Foundation Deposits in Ancient Mesopotamia* (New Haven, CT: Yale University Press, 1968). Prehistoric burials from Tepe Gawra are reported in Mitchell S. Rothman, *Tepe Gawra: The Evolution of a Small, Prehistoric Center in Northern Iraq* (Philadelphia: University of Pennsylvania, Museum of Archaeology and Anthropology, 2002). For the earliest appearances of lapis in Mesopotamia and Egypt, see Roger (P.R.S.) Moorey, *Ancient Mesopotamian Materials and Industries: The Archaeological Evidence* (Winona Lake, IN: Eisenbrauns, 1999) and also Paul

T. Nicholson and Ian Shaw (eds.), *Ancient Egyptian Materials and Technology* (Cambridge: Cambridge University Press, 2000).

The literature on trade and exchange in Neolithic societies is largely confined to specialist journals. For synthetic accounts dealing with the Near East, see David Wengrow, 'The Changing Face of Clay: Continuity and Change in the Transition from Village to Urban Life in the Near East', *Antiquity* 72 (1998): 783–95; *idem, The Archaeology of Early Egypt* (Cambridge: Cambridge University Press, 2006); and also Andrew G. Sherratt, 'Cash-Crops before Cash: Organic Consumables and Trade', in Chris Gosden and John G. Hather (eds.), *The Prehistory of Food: Appetites for Change* (London: Routledge, 1999), 13–34. A number of Sherratt's seminal essays on prehistoric trade are brought together in his *Economy and Society in Prehistoric Europe: Changing Perspectives* (Edinburgh: Edinburgh University Press, 1997); and see also 'Reviving the Grand Narrative: Archaeology and Long-Term Change', *Journal of European Archaeology* 3 (1995): 1–33.

Our understanding of the domestication of animals and plants in the 'Fertile Crescent', and of the subsequent spread of farming practices, is constantly shifting in the light of new data. Attempts at synthesis are often strongly conditioned by particular theoretical stances, with varying degrees of causality ascribed to social and environmental factors. Compare, for example, Jacques Cauvin, *The Birth of the Gods and the Origins of Agriculture* (Cambridge: Cambridge University Press, 2000);

and Peter Bellwood, *The First Farmers: The Origins of Agricultural Societies* (Malden, MA/Oxford: Blackwell, 2005). Much additional information can be found in David R. Harris (ed.), *The Origins and Spread of Agriculture and Pastoralism in Eurasia* (London: UCL Press, 1996) and in Sue Colledge and James Conolly (eds.), *The Origins and Spread of Domestic Plants in Southwest Asia and Europe* (Walnut Creek, CA: Left Coast Press, 2007). For early farming in Egypt and Sudan, see David Wengrow, *op. cit.* (2006); and also Peter Mitchell, *African Connections: An Archaeological Perspective on Africa and the Wider World* (Walnut Creek, CA: AltaMira, 2005).

Evidence for prehistoric maritime activity in the Eastern Mediterranean (including the spread of domesticates to Cyprus) and in the Persian Gulf is reviewed, respectively, by Cyprian Broodbank, 'The Origins and Early Development of Mediterranean Maritime Activity', *Journal of Mediterranean Archaeology* 19 (2006): 199–230; and Nicole Boivin and Dorian Q. Fuller, 'Shell Middens, Ships, and Seeds: Exploring Coastal Subsistence, Maritime Trade and the Dispersal of Domesticates in and around the Ancient Arabian Peninsula', *Journal of World Prehistory* 22 (2009): 113–80; and see also Robert Carter, 'Boat Remains and Maritime Trade in the Persian Gulf during the Sixth and Fifth Millennia BC', *Antiquity* 80 (2006): 52–63. Evidence for Neolithic dairying is presented in R. P. Evershed et al., 'Earliest Date for Milk Use in the Near East and Southeastern Europe Linked to Cattle Herding', *Nature* 455 (2008): 528–31.

For detailed discussion of Göbekli Tepe, see Klaus Schmidt, *Sie bauten die ersten Tempel: Das rätselhafte Heiligtum der Steinzeitjäger* (Munich: Beck, 2007); and for the role of ritual and ceremony in early farming societies, see Ian Hodder, *Çatalhöyük: The Leopard's Tale; Revealing the Mysteries of Turkey's Ancient 'Town'* (London: Thames and Hudson, 2006). Similar themes are explored for Egypt and Sudan in David Wengrow (2006), *op. cit.* Dorian Fuller and Michael Rowlands' innovative comparison of early food processing techniques across various parts of Africa and Asia (drawing upon primary research by Michèle Wollstonecroft) is germane to a number of the arguments presented in this book, and is to appear in a volume commemorating the work of Andrew Sherratt, as: 'Ingestion and Food Technologies—Maintaining Differences over the Long-Term in West, South and East Asia', in D. J. Bennet et al. (eds.), *Interweaving Worlds: Systemic Interaction in Eurasia, 7th to 1st Millennia BC* (Oxford: Oxbow Books, forthcoming).

Other works referred to include D. Edwards, 'Ancient Egypt in the Sudanese Middle Nile: A Case of Mistaken Identity?', in D. O'Connor and A. Reid (eds.), *Ancient Egypt in Africa* (London: UCL Press, 2003), 137–50; R. Haaland, 'Porridge and Pot, Bread and Oven: Food Ways and Symbolism in Africa and the Near East', *Cambridge Archaeological Journal* 17 (2007): 165–82; I. Hodder, *The Domestication of Europe* (Oxford: Blackwell, 1990); C. Lévi-Strauss, *The Savage Mind [La pensée sauvage]* (London: Facts on File, 1966). For interactions and exchanges between Neolithic societies, see also http://www.archatlas.dept.shef.ac.uk; for the site of Çatalhöyük, http://www.catalhoyuk.com; and for extensive object collections from prehistoric Egypt, and links to online learning resources, http://www.petrie.ucl.ac.uk

Chapter 4. The (First) Global Village

General overviews of the Ubaid period are provided in Petr Charvát, *Mesopotamia before History* (London: Routledge, 2002); Peter M. M. G. Akkermans and Glenn Schwartz, *The Archaeology of Syria: From Complex Hunter-Gatherers to Early Urban Societies, c.16,000–300 BC* (Cambridge: Cambridge University Press, 2003); and see also David Wengrow, 'The Changing Face of Clay: Continuity and Change in the Transition from Village to Urban Life in the Near East', *Antiquity* 72 (1998): 783–95; and Susan Pollock, *Ancient Mesopotamia. The Eden That Never Was* (Cambridge: Cambridge University Press, 1999). A careful evaluation of Ubaid-period maritime trade is provided by Robert Carter, 'Boat Remains and Maritime Trade in the Persian Gulf during the Sixth and Fifth Millennia BC', *Antiquity* 80 (2006): 52–63. For the 'dark millennium' in the Persian Gulf, see Adrian G. Parker and Andrew S. Goudie, 'Development of the Bronze Age Landscape in the Southeastern Arabian Gulf: New Evidence from a Buried Shell Midden in the Eastern Extremity of the Rub' al-Khali desert, Emirate of Ras al-Khaimah, U.A.E.', *Arabian Archaeology and Epigraphy* 18 (2007): 132–8; and for the formation of the Gulf waters since the end of the last Ice Age, see Kurt Lambeck, 'Shoreline Reconstructions for the Persian Gulf since the Last Glacial Maximum', *Earth and Planetary Science Letters* 142 (1996): 43–57.

Archaeological evidence for the beginnings of metallurgy is surveyed in Vincent C. Pigott (ed.), *The Archaeometallurgy of the Asian Old World* (Philadelphia: Museum University of Pennsylvania, 1999); and see also Roger (P.R.S.) Moorey, *Ancient Mesopotamian Materials and Industries: The Archaeological Evidence* (Winona Lake, IN: Eisenbrauns, 1999); Paul T. Nicholson and Ian Shaw (eds.), *Ancient Egyptian Materials and Technology* (Cambridge: Cambridge University Press, 2000); Evgenyi N. Chernykh, *Ancient Metallurgy in the USSR: The Early Metal* Age (Cambridge: Cambridge University Press, 1992); Thomas E. Levy, *Journey to the Copper Age* (San Diego: San Diego Museum of Man, 2007); and for Değirmentepe see K. Aslihan Yener, *The Domestication of Metals* (Leiden: Brill, 2000). The dissemination of tree-crop horticulture and woollen textiles is discussed in Andrew G. Sherratt, 'Cash-Crops before Cash: Organic Consumables and Trade', in Chris Gosden and John G. Hather (eds.), *The Prehistory of Food: Appetites for Change* (London: Routledge, 1999), 13–34; and see also Joy McCorriston, 'The Fibre Revolution: Textile Extensification, Alienation, and Social Stratification in Ancient Mesopotamia', *Current Anthropology* 38 (1997): 517–49. For tentative evidence of Neolithic fig domestication, see Mordechai Kislev et al., 'Early Domesticated Fig in the Jordan valley', *Science* 312 (5778): 1372–4, but also critical remarks by Simcha Lev-Yadun et al. in ibid. 314 (5806): 1683.

The early development of sealing practices is reviewed in Dominique Collon, *First Impressions: Cylinder Seals in the Ancient Near East* (London: British Museum, 1995), and *idem, 7000 Years of Seals* (London: British Museum, 1997). The evolution of cuneiform writing from clay tokens and other miniature objects is the subject of an extensive study by Denise Schmandt-Besserat, *Before Writing*, 2 vols. (Austin: University of Texas Press, 1992). Her work on this topic has, however, been heavily criticized on points of both logic and detail; for which, see Paul E. Zimansky in the *Journal of Field Archaeology* 20 (1993): 513–17.

Other works referred to include V. Gordon Childe, *The Bronze Age* (Cambridge: Cambridge University Press, 1930); *idem, Man Makes Himself* (London: Watts, 1936); M. Eliade, *The Forge and the Crucible* (London: Rider, 1978); R. Redfield, *The Primitive World and Its Transformations* (Ithaca, NY: Cornell University Press, 1953).

Chapter 5. Origin of Cities

A translation of 'The Sumerian King List', and general discussion of Mesopotamian historiography, can be found in Jean-Jacques Glassner's *Mesopotamian Chronicles* (Atlanta: Society of Biblical Literature, 2004). The story of *Enmerkar and the Lord of Aratta* is translated, with commentary, in Herman L. J. Vanstiphout, *Epics of Sumerian Kings: The Matter of Aratta* (Leiden: Brill, 2004).

The 'Uruk Expansion' has been a subject of intense debate among archaeologists for the past two decades. The discussion was set in motion principally by salvage excavations along the upper courses of the Euphrates and Tigris, which revealed closer connections to the Mesopotamian alluvium than previously suspected. Guillermo Algaze, *The Uruk World System: The Dynamics of Expansion of Early Mesopotamian Civilization* (Chicago: Chicago University Press, 1993) proposes an encompassing explanation for the wide distribution of Uruk-related material, drawing on Marxian analyses of the global spread of capitalism since the fifteenth century AD; and see now, *idem, Ancient Mesopotamia at the Dawn of Civilization: The Evolution of an Urban Landscape* (Chicago/London: University of Chicago Press, 2008). Other analyses of the transition to urban life in the fourth millennium BC emphasize local over trans-regional processes; see, for example, contributions in Mitchell S. Rothman (ed.), *Uruk Mesopotamia and Its Neighbors: Cross-Cultural Interactions in the Era of State Formation* (Oxford/Santa Fe, NM: James Currey; School of American Research, 2001). For an overview of the growth of urban life in the Indus Valley, see Gregory L. Possehl, *The Indus Civilization: A Contemporary Perspective* (Walnut Creek, CA/Oxford: AltaMira, 2002).

The Old Assyrian caravan trade with Kanesh is the subject of Klaas R. Veenhof, *Aspects of Old Assyrian Trade and Its Terminology* (Leiden: Brill, 1972). Innovations in traction and transport during the fourth millennium BC are discussed in Andrew G. Sherratt, *Economy and Society in Prehistoric Europe: Changing Perspectives* (Edinburgh: Edinburgh University Press, 1997), and *idem*, 'Animal traction and the Transformation of Europe' (available at http://www.archatlas.dept.shef.ac.uk/). The development of rotary techniques for seal manufacture and ceramics is reviewed in Roger (P.R.S.) Moorey, *Ancient Mesopotamian Materials and Industries: The Archaeological Evidence* (Winona Lake, IN: Eisenbrauns, 1999). For a survey of the earliest Mesopotamian writing, and its administrative context, see Hans Nissen et al., *Archaic Bookkeeping: Early Writing and Techniques of Economic Administration in the Ancient Near East* (Chicago/London: University of Chicago Press, 1993). Changing relationships between sealing practices, commodities, and consumption in the transition from Neolithic to urban life are discussed in David Wengrow, 'Prehistories of Commodity Branding', *Current Anthropology* 49 (2008): 7–34, with further references, and drawing comparisons with societies closer to home.

Other works referred to include P. Ariès, *Western Attitudes toward Death: From the Middle Ages to the Present*, trans. Patricia M. Ranum (London: Marion Boyars, 1994); W. Benjamin, 'The Work of Art in the Age of Mechanical Reproduction', in *Illuminations* (London: Pimlico, 1999 [1936]); B. R. Foster, *The Epic of Gilgamesh* (New York/London: Norton, 2001); A. McMahon and J. Oates, 'Excavations at Tell Brak 2006–7', *Iraq* 69 (2007): 145–71; D. Miller, 'Ideology and the Harappan Civilization', *Journal of Anthropological Archaeology* 4 (1985): 34–71; N. Postgate, *Early Mesopotamia: Society and*

Economy at the Dawn of History (New York: Routledge, 1996); D. Wengrow, *The Archaeology of Early Egypt: Social Transformations in North-East Africa, 10,000 to 2650 BC* (Cambridge: Cambridge University Press, 2006).

Chapter 6. From the Ganges to the Danube: The Bronze Age

The formation of the 'Eurasian metallogenic belt' is explained by Slobodan Janković, 'The Copper Deposits and Geotectonic Setting of the Tethyan Eurasian Metallogenic Belt', *Mineralium Deposita* 12 (1977): 37–47. For the origins of the Three-Age System, see Alain Schnapp, *The Discovery of the Past: The Origins of Archaeology* (London: British Museum Press, 1996).

For the growth of cities on the Iranian plateau, see Ali Hakemi, *Shahdad: Archaeological Excavations of a Bronze Age Center in Iran*, trans. S. M. S. Sajjadi (Rome: Ismeo, 1997); and Carl C. Lamberg-Karlovsky, *Beyond the Tigris and Euphrates: Bronze Age Civilizations* (Beer Sheva: Ben-Gurion University of the Negev Press, 1996). The 'Oxus' or 'Bactria-Margiana' civilization of Central Asia is discussed in Philip L. Kohl, *The Making of Bronze Age Eurasia* (Cambridge: Cambridge University Press, 2007); also Fredrik T. Hiebert, *Origins of the Bronze Age Oasis Civilization in Central Asia* (Cambridge, MA: Peabody Museum of Archaeology and Ethnology, Harvard University, 1994). A survey of early urban development in the Persian Gulf is provided by Harriet Crawford, *Dilmun and Its Gulf Neighbors* (Cambridge:

Cambridge University Press, 1998). Trade relations between these and adjacent areas are reviewed in Shereen Ratnagar, *Trading Encounters: From the Euphrates to the Indus in the Bronze Age* (New Delhi/Oxford: Oxford University Press, 2004). For metrological standards, see Alfredo Mederos and Carl C. Lamberg-Karlovsky, 'Converting Currencies in the Old World', *Nature* 411 (2001): 437; and also Lorenz Rahmstorf, 'The Concept of Weighing during the Bronze Age in the Aegean, the Near East and Europe', in I. Morley and C. Renfrew (eds), *The Archaeology of Measurement: Comprehending Heaven, Earth and Time in Ancient Societies* (Cambridge: Cambridge University Press, 2009).

The early development of bronze technology, and its selective adoption across the western Old World, is the subject of a study by Lloyd Weeks, *Early Metallurgy of the Persian Gulf: Technology, Trade, and the Bronze Age World* (Boston/Leiden: Brill, 2003). Ornamental uses of bronze, from Sumer to the Aegean, are illustrated and discussed in Joan Aruz (ed.), *Art of the First Cities* (New York: Metropolitan Museum of Art; New Haven, CT/London: Yale University Press, 2003). Textual evidence for the stockpiling and circulation of silver in standard units is presented in Giovanni Pettinato, *Ebla: A New Look at History* (Baltimore: Johns Hopkins University Press, 1991). For the importance of temples as repositories of wealth and guarantors of value, see Morris Silver, *Economic Structures of the Ancient Near East* (London: Croom Helm, 1985); and essays in Edward Lipinski (ed.), *State and Temple Economy in the Ancient*

Near East (Leuven: Departement Oriëntalistiek, 1979). The role of private enterprise in Bronze Age economies is beyond the scope of this book, but see Michael Hudson and Baruch A. Levine, *Privatization in the Ancient Near East and Classical World* (Cambridge, MA: Peabody Museum of Archaeology and Ethnology, 1996).

The significance of Bronze Age metal hoards in temperate Europe is considered in Anthony F. Harding, *European Societies in the Bronze Age* (Cambridge: Cambridge University Press, 2002), and for the Ganges-Yamuna copper hoards, see Paul Yule, 'The Copper Hoards of Northern India', *Expedition* 39 (1997): 22–32. The deposition of metalwork within tombs and burials in Oman, Afghanistan, the Caucasus, and Luristan is documented largely in specialist sources, select examples of which are included below ('other works'). Regrettably few of these finds were recovered during scientific excavations; many have entered the antiquities market from unknown or anecdotal sources, and their date and provenance remain a matter of supposition.

The temple deposits at Byblos and Ugarit are illustrated in Claude Doumet-Serhal (ed.), *Decade: A Decade of Archaeology and History in Lebanon* (Beirut: Lebanese British Friends of the National Museum, 2004). For later Eurasian examples of metal-hoarding on the margins of urban expansion, see Joan Aruz (ed.), *The Golden Deer of Eurasia: Scythian and Sarmatian Treasures from the Russian Steppes* (New York: Metropolitan Museum of Art, 2000); Peter Spufford, *Money and Its Use in Medieval Europe* (Cambridge: Cambridge University Press,

1987). The *Potlatch* ceremony is discussed by Marcel Mauss, *The Gift: The Form and Reason for Exchange in Archaic Societies*, trans. from 1925 original by W. D. Halls (London: Routledge, 2002); and see also Maurice Godelier, *The Enigma of the Gift*, trans. Nora Scott (Chicago: University of Chicago Press, 1999).

Other works referred to include P. Beaujard, 'The Indian Ocean in Eurasian and African World-Systems before the Sixteenth Century', *Journal of World History* 16(4) (2005): 411–65; D. Boucher et al. (eds), (2005) *The Philosophy of Enchantment: Studies in Folktale, Cultural Criticism, and Anthropology* (Oxford: Oxford University Press, 2005); J. S. Cooper, *Presargonic Inscriptions* (New Haven, CT: American Oriental Society; Winona Lake, IN: Eisenbrauns, 1986); C. Edens, 'Transcaucasia at the End of the Early Bronze Age', *Bulletin of the American Schools of Oriental Research* 299/300 (1995): 53–64; A. George, *House Most High: The Temples of Ancient Mesopotamia* (Winona Lake, IN: Eisenbrauns, 1993); E. Haerinck and B. Overlaet, *Bani Surmah: An Early Bronze Age Graveyard in Pusht-i Kuh, Luristan* (Leuven: Peeters, 2006); S. Küchler, 'Sacrificial Economy and Its Objects', *Journal of Material Culture* 2 (1997): 39–60; G. Philip, 'Cypriot Bronzework in the Levantine World: Conservatism, Innovation and Social Change', *Journal of Mediterranean Archaeology* 4(1) (1991): 59–107; V. I. Sarianidi, *Die Kunst des alten Afghanistan: Architektur, Keramik, Siegel: Kunstwerke aus Stein und Metall* (Weinheim: VCH, 1986); C. F. A. Schaeffer, 'Ex Occidente Ars', in *Ugaritica VII* (Paris:

Paul Geuthner; Leiden: Brill, 1978), 475–551; T. Stech and V. Pigott, 'The Metals Trade in Southwest Asia in the Third Millennium BC', *Iraq* 48 (1986): 39–64; C. P. Thornton, 'The Emergence of Complex Metallurgy on the Iranian Plateau: Escaping the Levantine Paradigm', *Journal of World Prehistory* 22 (2009): 301–27; G. Weisgerber and P. Yule, 'The First Metal Hoard in Oman', in K. Frifelt and P. Sørensen (eds.), *South Asian Archaeology 1985* (London: Curzon Press, 1989), 60–1. Translations of the 'Lament for Ur' and other Sumerian texts are available in J. A. Black et al., *The Electronic Text Corpus of Sumerian Literature* (Oxford, 1998–2006; http://etcsl.orinst.ox.ac.uk/).

Chapter 7. Cosmology and Commerce

Attitudes to divine images in ancient Mesopotamia and Egypt (as well as other regions) are compared in Michael B. Dick (ed.), *Born in Heaven, Made on Earth: The Making of the Cult Image in the Ancient Near East* (Winona Lake, IN: Eisenbrauns, 1999); and see also Victor Hurowitz, 'What Goes in Is What Comes out: Materials for Creating Cult Statues', in Gary M. Beckman and Theodore J. Lewis (eds.), *Text, Artifact, and Image: Revealing Ancient Israelite Religion* (Providence, RI: Brown Judaic Studies, 2006). Cult images from Egypt are illustrated and discussed in Marsha Hill (ed.), *Gifts for the Gods: Images from Egyptian Temples* (New York: Metropolitan Museum of Art; New Haven, CT/ London: Yale University Press, 2007).

'Atrahasis' and the 'Epic of Creation' are translated in Stephanie Dalley, *Myths from Mesopotamia: Creation, the Flood, Gilgamesh, and Others* (Oxford/New York: Oxford University Press, 2000); and for Egyptian cosmology, see James P. Allen, *Genesis in Egypt: The Philosophy of Ancient Egyptian Creation Accounts* (New Haven, CT: Yale University Press, 1988). The Mesopotamian 'Opening of the Mouth' ritual is analysed in depth by Christopher Walker and Michael Dick, *The Induction of the Cult Image in Ancient Mesopotamia* (University of Helsinki: Institute for Asian and African Studies, 2001); and its Egyptian counterpart by Hans-W. Fischer-Elfert, *Die Vision von der Statue im Stein: Studien zum altägyptischen Mundöffnungsritual* (Heidelberg: Universitäts Verlag, 1998). A more accessible account can be found in John H. Taylor, *Death and the Afterlife in Ancient Egypt* (London: British Museum, 2001). Illuminating comparisons are drawn by Irene Winter, 'Opening the Eyes and Opening the Mouth: The Utility of Comparing Images in Worship in India and the Ancient Near East', in M. W. Meister (ed.), *Ethnography and Personhood: Notes from the Field* (Jaipur/New Delhi: Rawat, 2000), 129–62.

For the feeding of cult statues, see contributions in Jan Quaegebeur, *Ritual and Sacrifice in the Ancient Near East* (Leuven: Peeters, 1993); and also Jean Bottéro, *The Oldest Cuisine in the World: Cooking in Mesopotamia*, trans. T. L. Fagan (Chicago/London: University of Chicago Press, 2004); Nicholas Postgate, *Early Mesopotamia: Society and Economy at the Dawn of History* (New York: Routledge, 1996), 119–22; Ursula Verhoeven, *Grillen, Kochen, Backen im Alltag und in Ritual Altägyptens: ein Lexikographischer Beitrag* (Bruxelles: Fondation Égyptologique Reine Élisabeth, 1984). A. Leo Oppenheim's 'The Care and Feeding of the Gods' in his *Ancient Mesopotamia: Portrait of a Dead Civilization* (Chicago/London: University of Chicago Press, 1977), remains fundamental. And for wider Mediterranean comparisons, see Marcel Detienne and Jean-Pierre Vernant, *The Cuisine of Sacrifice among the Greeks* (Chicago/London: University of Chicago Press, 1989).

Other works referred to include Maurice Godelier, *The Enigma of the Gift*, trans. Nora Scott (Chicago: University of Chicago Press, 1999); S. N. Kramer, *History Begins at Sumer* (London: Thames and Hudson, 1961).

Chapter 8. The Labours of Kingship

For reasons of brevity, this book presents a normative view of Mesopotamian and Egyptian kingship. I have not, for instance, discussed exceptional cases of divine rulers in Mesopotamia, for which see the contributions by Piotr Michalwoski and Irene Winter in Nicole Brisch et al. (eds), *Religion and Power: Divine Kingship in the Ancient World and Beyond* (Chicago: Oriental Institute Seminars, no. 4, 2008).

The 'Amarna Letters, discovered in Egypt over a century ago, comprise diplomatic correspondence between the ruling houses of the ancient Near East, recorded in Akkadian cuneiform. They reveal a formalized pattern of interpalatial relationships extending between Egypt, Mesopotamia, and surrounding regions (see Raymond Cohen and Raymond Westbrook (eds), *Amarna Diplomacy: The Beginnings of International Relations* (Baltimore: Johns Hopkins University Press, 2000). For further discussion of Mesopotamian legal codes and their relationship to juridical practice, see Norman Yoffee, *Myths of the Archaic State* (Cambridge: Cambridge University Press), 100–12. A detailed inventory of related sources is provided by Raymond Westbrook, *A History of Ancient Near Eastern Law* (Leiden: Brill, 2003).

For further discussion of early Mesopotamian sculpture, including the plaques of Ur-Nanshe, see Henri Frankfort, *The Art and Architecture of the Ancient Orient*, 5th edn. (New Haven, CT/London: Yale University Press, 1996); and for the monuments of Ur-Namma, Jeanny V. Canby, *The Ur-nammu Stela* (Philadelphia: University of Pennsylvania Museum of Archaeology and Anthropology, 2001). Dietz O. Edzard, *Gudea and His Dynasty* (Toronto: University of Toronto Press, 1997) gives a full edition of Gudea's temple hymn; and for further discussion, see Richard Averbeck, 'Sumer, the Bible, and Comparative Method: Historiography and Temple Building', in M. W. Chavalas and K. Lawson Younger Jr. (eds.), *Mesopotamia and the Bible: Comparative Explorations* (London: Sheffield Academic Press, 2002), 88–125. Detailed discussion of Mesopotamian temple architecture can be found in Henri Frankfort, *Pre-Sargonid Temples in the Diyala Region* (Chicago: University of Chicago Press, 1942), and for a more accessible review see his *Art and Architecture, op. cit.*, 42–5. Ritual uses of incense in Mesopotamia and Egypt are compared and contrasted in Kjeld Nielsen, *Incense in Ancient Israel* (Leiden: Brill, 1986).

The unification of the Egyptian kingdom and the role of interregional contacts in that process are the subject of David Wengrow, *The Archaeology of Early Egypt: Social Transformations in North-East Africa, 10,000 to 2650 BC* (Cambridge: Cambridge University Press, 2006). The development of pyramid complexes is traced into the Old Kingdom and beyond by I. E. S. Edwards, *The Pyramids of Egypt*, rev. edn. (London: Penguin, 1993); and see also Mark Lehner's *The Complete Pyramids* (London: Thames and Hudson, 1997). For 'pyramid towns' and associated mortuary cults, see Barry Kemp's *Ancient Egypt: Anatomy of a Civilization*, 2nd edn. (London: Routledge, 2006). The workings of the *phyle* system are analysed by Ann Macy Roth, *Egyptian Phyles in the Old Kingdom: The Evolution of a System of Social Organization* (Chicago: Oriental Institute of the University of Chicago, 1991). Mummification, the role of cult statues, and the development of funerary texts in Egyptian tombs are conveniently reviewed in John H. Taylor's *Death and the Afterlife in Ancient Egypt* (London: British Museum Press, 2001); and see also Sue D'Auria et al., *Mummies and Magic: The Funerary Arts of Ancient Egypt* (Boston: Museum of Fine Arts, 1988). Christopher Eyre, *The Cannibal Hymn* (Liverpool: Liverpool University Press, 2002), provides a detailed study of the role of meat sacrifice and consumption in the Pyramid Texts.

Other works referred to include B. Anderson, *Imagined Communities* (London/New York: Verso, 1991); J. Assmann, *The Search for God in Ancient Egypt*, trans. D. Lorton (Ithaca, NY: Cornell University Press, 2001); J. Bottéro, *The Oldest Cuisine in the World: Cooking in Mesopotamia*, trans. T. L. Fagan (Chicago/London: University of Chicago Press, 2004); H. Frankfort, *Kingship and the Gods: A Study of Ancient Near Eastern Religion as the Integration of Society and Nature* (Chicago: University of Chicago Press, 1948); W. Helck, *Untersuchungen zu den Beamtentiteln des ägyptischen Alten Reiches* (Glückstadt/New York: J. J. Augustin, 1954); A. J. Mayer, *The Persistence of the Old Regime: Europe to the Great War* (New York: Pantheon, 1981); D. O'Connor, 'Context, Function and Program: Understanding Ceremonial Slate Palettes', *Journal of the American Research Center in Egypt* 39 (2002), 5–25; B. Wells, 'Law and Practice', in D. C. Snell (ed.), *A Companion to the Ancient Near East* (Oxford: Blackwell, 2005); William II, German Emperor, *Das Königtum in alten Mesopotamien* (Berlin: Walter de Gruyter, 1938). Current investigations on the Giza plateau are documented at http://www.aeraweb.org/gpmp_home.asp, with links to related projects.

Chapter 9. Enlightenment From a Dark Source

For an authoritative treatment of the relationship between antiquarianism and constitutional law in northern Europe, see John G. A. Pocock, *The Ancient*

Constitution and the Feudal Law: A Study of English Historical Thought in the Seventeenth Century (Cambridge: Cambridge University Press, 1957). Alain Schnapp, *The Discovery of the Past: The Origins of Archaeology* (London: British Museum Press, 1996), provides an illustrated survey of the development of scientific prehistory in its wider social and political contexts, and Philip Schwyzer offers an engaging analysis of the emergence of the 'archaeological imagination' as an outcome of tensions in early modern society: *Archaeologies of English Renaissance Literature* (Oxford: Oxford University Press, 2007). Isaac Newton's writings on the ancient Near East can be viewed at http://www.newtonproject.sussex.ac.uk. The Chicago tympanum is further considered by Mogens Larsen, 'Orientalism and Near Eastern Archaeology', in Daniel Miller et al. (eds.), *Domination and Resistance* (London: Unwin Hyman, 1989), 229–39.

Other works referred to include J. H. Breasted, *The Dawn of Conscience* (New York/London: Scribner, 1934); V. Gordon Childe, *New Light on the Most Ancient East: The Oriental Prelude to European Prehistory* (London: K. Paul, Trench, Trubner, 1934); *idem, Man Makes Himself* (London: Watts, 1936); E. Said, *Orientalism: Western Conceptions of the Orient*, 4th edn. (London: Penguin, 1995).

Chapter 10. Ruined Regimes: Egypt at the Revolution

Changing displays and adaptations of ancient Egyptian imagery in France before and after the Revolution are richly documented in James S. Curl, *Egyptomania: The Egyptian Revival* (Manchester: Manchester University Press, 1994); and see also Jean-Marcel Humbert, *L'Égypte à Paris* (Paris: Action Artistique de la Ville de Paris, 1997); *idem* et al., *Egyptomania: Egypt in Western Art, 1730–1930* (Ottawa: National Gallery of Canada; Paris: Réunion des Musées Nationaux, 1994). A number of excellent studies deal with the early development of the Louvre, among them Cecil Gould, *Trophy of Conquest: The Musée Napoleon and the Creation of the Louvre* (London: Faber and Faber, 1965); Andreu Guillemette et al., *L'Égypte ancienne au Louvre* (Paris: Hachette, 1997); Andrew McClellan, *Inventing the Louvre: Art, Politics, and the Origins of the Modern Museum in Eighteenth-Century Paris* (Cambridge: Cambridge University Press, 1994). More detailed discussion of the Napoleonic expedition to Egypt, and its consequences, is found in Edward Said, *Orientalism: Western Conceptions of the Orient*, 4th edn. (London: Penguin, 1995); Patrice Bret, *L'éxpedition d'Égypte: une entreprise des lumières, 1798–1801* (Paris: Technique et Documentation, 1999); Terence M. Russell, *The Discovery of Egypt: Vivant Denon's Travels with Napoleon's Army* (Stroud: Sutton, 2005). For the importance of female icons in revolutionary art and ideology, see Maurice Agulhon, *Marianne into Battle: Republican Imagery and Symbolism in France, 1789–1880*, trans. Janet Lloyd (Cambridge: Cambridge University Press, 1981).

Other works referred to include J. Assmann, *Moses the Egyptian: The Memory of Egypt in Western Monotheism*

(Cambridge, MA/London: Harvard University Press, 1997); P. Hughes, 'Ruins of Time: Estranging History and Ethnology in the Enlightenment and After', in D. O. Hughes and T. R. Trautmann (eds.), *Time: Histories and Ethnologies* (Ann Arbor: University of Michigan Press, 1995), 269–90; J. Michelet, *History of the French Revolution*, trans. C. Cocks (Chicago/London: University of Chicago Press, 1967 [1879–80]); J-M. Moiret, *Memories of Napoleon's Egyptian Expedition*, trans. Rosmary Brindle (London: Greenhill, 2001 [1798–1801]); M. Ozouf, *Festivals and the French Revolution*, trans. Alan Sheridan (Cambridge, MA/London: Harvard University Press, 1988); C. F. Volney, *The Ruins, or, Meditation on the Revolutions of Empires* (Baltimore: Classic Press, 1991 [1890; 1791]).

PICTURE
ACKNOWLEDGEMENTS

Krzysztof Ciałowicz and the Tell el-Farkha Expedition: 1; National Museum, Damascus/Erich Lessing/ akg-images: 2; Institute of Archaeology, University College London: 3; Ashmolean Museum, University of Oxford/The Bridgeman Art Library: 4; The Petrie Museum, University College London: 5; The Trustees Of The British Museum: 6; The Israel Museum, Jerusalem/The Bridgeman Art Library: 7; after H. Frankfort, *Cylinder Seals* (London: Macmillan, 1938); P. Amiet, *La glyptique mésopotamienne archaïque* (Paris: CNRS, 1980): 8; Augusta McMahon and the Tell Brak Expedition: 9; Aleppo Museum/Philippe Maillard/ akg-images: 10; Werner Forman Archive: 11; Cuneiform Digital Library/Ashmolean Museum, University of Oxford: 12; Musée du Louvre Paris/Gianni Dagli Orti/ The Art Archive: 13; after *Abhandlungen der Preussichen Akademie der Wissenschaften* 13 (1936); W. B. Emery, *The Tomb of Hemaka* (Cairo: Government Press, 1938): 14; after R. Lepsius, *Denkmäler aus Ägypten und Äthiopien* (Leipzig: Hinrichs, 1913): 15; Ancient Egypt Research Associates: 16; Erich Lessing/akg-images: 17; Special Collections Research Center, University of Chicago Library (apf2-05517): 18; Private collection/Dahesh Museum of Art, New York: 19; Musée d'art moderne Richard Anacréon, Granville, France/akg-images: 20.

INDEX